ISLANDS OF REALITY

ISLANDS OF REALITY

the souls on-going journey

J J J

© 2016 J J J
All rights reserved.

ISBN-13: 9781533375346
ISBN-10: 1533375348

Table of Contents

Foreword · vii

Chapter 1	Introduction ·	1
Chapter 2	About the Council ·	5
Chapter 3	The Effects of Mass Media on the Esoteric · · · · · · · · · · ·	10
Chapter 4	What Is the Purpose of the Council? · · · · · · · · · · · · · ·	14
Chapter 5	Self-Enlightenment ·	19
Chapter 6	Synchronicities ·	24
Chapter 7	Making the Connection ·	27
Chapter 8	The Soul's Balance ·	30
Chapter 9	Perception and Understanding · · · · · · · · · · · · · · · · ·	36
Chapter 10	The Higher Conscience ·	39
Chapter 11	Connection to Source ·	44
Chapter 12	Meditative States of Understanding · · · · · · · · · · · · ·	49
Chapter 13	Principles of Attraction ·	55
Chapter 14	The Acceptance of All ·	58
Chapter 15	Question Time ·	62

Foreword

This book is dedicated to each and every soul, in whatever form and in whatever time and place it currently finds itself. Whether you are yet to awaken, have already awakened, or have been awake for some time, remember always that we are each a part of a very special whole. We have much to learn, much to share, and much to experience.

The journey of the soul while in this domain is certainly not an easy one. Yet it is not supposed or meant to be. Often, specific to this current reality, souls seeking awakening and connection have come up against and have encountered much negativity, sometimes physical, not only in the present but also in the past, when trying to share with others their own thoughts in relation to their own perceptions of this reality.

Yet in the face of such hostility, those souls have continued to keep their own truths held very close and very dear to their own hearts. This takes courage, commitment, determination, and perhaps most importantly, faith, love, and hope. To not let go of your own instinctive intuitions, even in the face of much negativity, tests even the most determined of souls.

There is no doubting that this cycle of life, as we experience it, can be extremely testing and tiresome at times. Often, thoughts of giving up are a natural part of reconnecting to the infinite and divine source of that which we feel and sense in our hearts.

If indeed you have encountered or are encountering such thoughts, then my message to you would be to not give up. Sometimes the burden of this reality can load a weight onto our shoulders, which at times feels too heavy to carry. Yet in the end, our ultimate destination appears to be the same, according to the path that you take along your own journey. It's how you make this journey and the experiences that you have while undertaking this journey that count.

There is, without a doubt, a shift of consciousness that is underway and has been underway for some time. There are those within this time and place who have attempted to speed up this shift. And conversely, there are those who have attempted to slow down or halt this shift for reasons according to their own perceptions of our surroundings.

However, the shift that occurs now cannot be prevented. It could be disrupted, yes. It could also still be hindered. But even they who have sought to keep buried the truth understand that the truth cannot be kept buried indefinitely or forever.

Personally, I do not believe that as of May 2016, when this book was finished, humanity, collectively at least, is ready to bear witness to the truths that reside beyond the veil. I also do not believe, collectively at least, that mass disclosure in relation to the presence of intelligences not domicile on this sphere would benefit this civilization in its current stage of collective awareness, development, and understanding.

Of course, that time shall come. And of course, there are still those present at this moment in time who are able to embrace the many, many hidden aspects of this temporary reality. Yet for the moment at least, such individuals undertake their own journeys of discovery in a manner that suits them, out of the public eye, while the many, many layers of this civilization continue to work according to that which they feel is correct, according to their own perceptions of this existence—their own islands of reality.

In the not too distant future, there will be a convergence of timelines, which means that this civilization will indeed be ready to be shown that which many of you feel. How soon will this time come? Well, that depends on the balance and understanding of every soul that inhabits a cycle of experience during this time and place. Perhaps a way of looking at it is that you would not take a fish out of the sea and take it to the moon, as the moon would not make any sense to it. Rather, the journey—in this example, to the moon—must be initiated and undertaken by the individual soul.

There are many markers along your path, which can point you in a direction that will resonate best with your own soul. However, in order to find such markers, which are unique to you, you must first gain an inner balance, which will enable the markers along your path to make themselves known to you.

I hope that in some way, this book can assist you to find alignment with the markers of your own path. You are never alone on your journey, even when it feels as if you are. To venture forward toward a united understanding for the benefit of all, you must first gain an understanding of what really is the essence of your own reality.

We desire to understand and experience, because such an understanding and such experiences are such a vital chapter in the onward journey of the soul. So go forth to experience, to understand, to love, and to learn. Never give up on hope, for hope shall never give up on you. Never abandon love, because love will never abandon you. Never lose faith, because faith will never lose you, even as you voyage through the remotest parts of the ocean of infinite experience.

And when the inevitable storms that come find you, or you them, look out onto the horizon and feel the warmth, the love, and the harmony of that which awaits us all. For eventually, the storm shall pass, and in its wake the dawn of a new beginning shall begin.

Always follow your heart, and always trust your instincts. May peace, harmony, and balance be with your soul, both on this journey and on those that are to come.

1

Introduction

Thank you for taking an interest in this book. Even if it helps or assists just one soul to realize its true and full potential by finding and connecting to its own inner self and thus, in doing so, to therefore reach the goals of its own path by helping to index the many feelings and emotions that often accompany an awoken state of mind, then this book will have achieved its objective and goal.

Many people are starting to become aware of a reality that goes way beyond that which general society is aware or accepting of. As an example, there are many souls that feel a deep and intimate resonance with their surroundings in a manner that gives them a new understanding in relation to their own perceptions: light workers, star seeds, indigo children, and empaths, plus many more. There is no denying that more and more people see themselves as more than just physical beings who live for a number of years and then just disappear and cease to be.

About a year ago, I formed an organization that is called the Council of Enlightened. One of the many purposes in relation to the formation of this organization was to bring together people from all over the world who each share in common a perception and awareness of this reality that goes way beyond the mere physical boundaries of what we can see with our own eyes.

I must first point out and affirm that the Council of Enlightened and its members do not claim to be fully or completely enlightened. Indeed,

I do not think that full enlightenment, not just as to the mysteries of this domain but also as to the mysteries of ALL domains, is even possible during this cycle of experience, mainly because I have a deep sense and feeling that such abilities and detailed perceptions are not our primary reason for being here, in this time and place.

However, people can indeed be at, or achieve, various levels of enlightenment relative to their own perceptions of their own realities. For example, you may already be open to the suggestion and notion that the soul does not die. Or perhaps maybe you believe that animals also have souls just as we do, but that they are having an experience that differs quite fundamentally and significantly from that which our physical bodies can offer and afford to us, because the purposes of their own journeys are quite different from our own. Or you may be enlightened as to the sense that there is more to this particular reality than what meets the physical senses of touch, smell, seeing, and hearing (among others).

Or maybe you are enlightened as to the existence of intelligences that are not domicile on this planet, and perhaps you have an understanding as to the reason and rationale behind their desire not to engage in activities conducive to mass disclosure at this moment in time.

Indeed, the point of the questions and answers that are at the end of this book are to help to perhaps give credence to your own thoughts and perceptions about things, which you may not have yet had the chance to share with those around you, maybe owing in part to the fact that those around you may not be ready or willing to listen to and accept such thoughts, experiences, views, and perceptions. Having an awareness about something that you feel rather than what you see but not having the ability to share such thoughts can be a very frustrating and often isolating affair.

So I do sincerely encourage you to keep your mind and perception open, while reading this book, as to what a collective of aware souls, all at various and different stages of understanding and perception, may indeed bring to your own current understanding and perception. Why?

Well, I guess that perhaps in doing so, it might open doors of perspectives that have been closed for some time. Or if such doors are already open, then perhaps this book will assist you in opening additional such doors, which perhaps you had not even considered before.

In truth, according to my own perception, there are no right and therefore no wrong answers to many of the questions that are presented in this book. The guidance of your own instinct, for as long as you are in tune with it, shall no doubt aid you in gaining a sense of what does and what does not resonate with you in this book.

Becoming aware can indeed be a volatile, emotional, and lonely affair. In my own example, not only do none of my family and friends know about this particular side of me that I am about to share with you, but they also do not know about the fact that I am writing this book. Why? Well, I think that solitude can be a useful thing when trying to find answers to very deep and very personal questions.

Yet for those who do desire to connect with like-minded individuals, then this is one of the reasons as to why the Council of Enlightened has been formed and why it is here. In forming the council, the hope is that its members can exchange thoughts, ideas, experiences, and perceptions in an open and free way, and that those involved in such exchanges can also become more aware to subjects or thoughts that perhaps they may not have previously considered.

I would also like to extend my personal thanks and gratitude to each member from within the council who shared with me his or her own response to the questions that were posed. Showing your inner side, even in a virtual sense, can be quite difficult, yet those who did share such responses kept their answers pure and without fear of ridicule because indeed the council itself is formed of members who already indicated such openness and understanding during their initial vetting before joining the council.

This book is dedicated to all souls, regardless of form, presence, or understanding, both who are aware and who are yet to find their own awareness. Yet such truths shall, at some point, find each soul as it continues on its onward journey of self-discovery, awareness, and connection to that which is responsible for us being here.

Regardless of where you are, what your situation is, or what faces you within this cycle of experience, never give up on faith, love, and hope, for such things form the vital part of the infinite whole.

2

About the Council

The Council of Enlightened consists of a group of souls from all over the globe who are all, in their own unique ways, aware. That is to say, each member has become aware of his or her physical surroundings in a manner and with a perception that lends itself to an acceptance of the notion that all possible outcomes and eventualities are indeed possible. I guess that you could call it an acceptance of all, which is covered in brief later on in this book.

That is to say, we do not dismiss or discredit anything, because anything is possible and we understand it to be this way. We have become effectively detached from a method and tradition of thinking that considers or acknowledges only that which can be observed with the physical eye, and perhaps the physical senses, as existing.

We acknowledge and accept all teachings and beliefs, yet we allow our own souls' perceptions to determine our own and individual truths. We form our understandings from both the direct and indirect experiences that we have had and that we are yet to have that lie on the unique and individual paths before us all.

What this means is that the council functions as an information exchange between people who have different levels of understanding and perception. This free flow of information, thinking, and ideas creates a community whose heart is concerned only with exploration and understanding. We refrain from discussing politics or talking about specific religions because such things are dependent upon the beliefs of the individual, and we seek not to change or alter such beliefs. We prefer instead to learn more about that which is behind our presence here, in this time and in this place.

Indeed, before any new potential member of the council joins us, he or she is asked two very specific questions, both of which are worded for an equally specific purpose. There is no right or wrong answer to these questions; rather the answers given allow me to understand whether the soul behind the physical body is ready to engage in and with a collective of individuals whose aim is concerned only with a greater understanding about the unseen, the unheard, and indeed the unknown, regardless of the polarity of the soul (i.e., whether the soul of the individual is concerned with service to self or service to others, or perhaps a mixture of the two).

This initiation, for want of a better word, is important because my aim in setting up the council was, in part, to voyage into the unknown realms of esoteric discovery, and such a task cannot be undertaken without ensuring that those who are party to such discussions and have an open and understanding mind. To tell someone that his or her opinion or perception is wrong (according to one's own opinion and perception) acts only to bury one's head deeper into the sands of slumber, which much of society has been buried under for so many years. For me personally, I never dismiss anything that I am told or shown. Rather, I trust my own instinct and indeed my intuition to inform me as to which information is and is not relevant to my particular path during this particular lifetime or, as I like to call it, cycle of experience.

I am not what I would call an author. Indeed, at school, English was one of those subjects that my naïve young mind thought that I did not need to pay too much attention to. "I am English," I thought, "so why do I need to pay attention in English classes?" Hindsight is a wonderful thing. So with that said, I must apologize in advance for the grammatical errors that you may encounter. However, I would much prefer the reader to digest and absorb that which is written below and see whether any of it resonates with your own soul. If it does, then great. If it does not, then worry not. It does not make you any less of an awoken mind if this book does not resonate with you. Perhaps in the future, it will.

I have also not sought to correct any grammatical errors that have been made by those within the council in relation to the answers that they gave to specific questions that can be found toward the end of this book. To tamper, alter, or change their words, I feel, would be to alter their responses and thus dilute the purity of their communication. After all, written words are only one means of communication. I would prefer readers to allow their inner feelings to embrace and explore the content of this book.

Whether you are in a heightened state of awareness, or whether this faculty of awareness is yet to find you, or you it, know that your soul is not and never was alone. The journey of your divine soul here, on this sphere, in your current physical body, can indeed be a painful and negative journey. However, as is often the way, there is an opposite of the negative, and indeed there is a balance between the two polarities of positive and negative. Personally, I try to maintain a balance between the two polarities of positive and negative, allowing both negative and positive experiences to find my soul yet not allowing my soul or its balance to become unduly displaced because of them.

I personally like to think of the physical body as a boat on a sea of experience. Each wave before you shall move you and affect you in a different way. Some waves, or experiences, will take you up, and some will, of course, take you down. Yet your soul, being at the helm of this boat, can steer your vessel according to the route that it so desires and the experiences that it feels drawn to. And regardless of the sea state, or condition of the sea, for as long as you look after and maintain your vessel and do not steer it into a storm, then it shall be able to continue to navigate you through this sea of metaphorical experience.

Personally, I do not think it is possible to have a journey here that is 100 percent positive, or indeed 100 percent negative, although owing to the energies associated with it, the latter can sometimes feel the more prominent force during your cycle of experience in this particular incarnation upon this particular sphere. The soul constantly meanders between the effects of positive energy and the effects of negative energy. The often-arduous task is often trying to find that state of equilibrium and balance between both the positive and the negative.

All events during your cycle of life within this realm, according to your own perception, can indeed perhaps lead to a greater sense of understanding and awareness. And this is one of the vital keys to a greater understanding and thus a greater awareness: the acceptance of all possibilities and potential outcomes. Accepting all possibilities and outcomes to all potential situations does not necessarily mean that you need to agree with all such possibilities and perceptions as they are presented to you. Rather, with acceptance comes a greater sense of understanding by applying the principles behind the possibilities that lead to the events or experiences.

As an example, if I said to you that by going a hundred miles out to sea on a rickety old boat to a nonparticular uninhabited island, you would find, once you arrive at your destination, proof of extraterrestrial intelligence, then you may just think that I am talking nonsense, as there is no such thing as extraterrestrial intelligence (according to your own perception). But what if you listened to this advice, knowing that it did not resonate with your current understanding and perception, but regardless you decided to undertake this voyage for yourself owing to a deep feeling from within your conscience that, for reasons that may not be apparent, drew you to undertake this voyage? Imagine that you do indeed head off in your boat and that during your passage, you encounter many ferocious storms and heavy seas.

At times during this voyage, you feel like giving up and going back to what you know, the relative safety and routine of your day-to-day activity back on shore. Yet something deep within your own conscience that is affected not by direct external influence motivates you to carry on and head deeper into the storm in order to arrive at your destination.

This something inside of you gently persuades you to continue forward unabated. This instinctive and familiar voice of your inner intuition and innate understanding has been with you ever since you can remember.

Even during the most testing of times of this short voyage, you do not give up. You have hope that at your destination, you will find what you are looking for or what you have been told to expect. You have faith in your vessel being able to get you to where you want to go. You feel love and passion for the energy of nature that surrounds your vessel even when it feels as though such energy and nature could be responsible for the capsizing of your vessel.

Then, after several long and turbulent days, you arrive at this small island a hundred miles offshore. You swim onto the island and explore it for several long days, yet you find no tangible proof of that extraterrestrial civilization that was promised to you. Yet you still know that there was a reason for coming out to this small island, and thus you do not let go of or give up on this sense of deep-seated hope. You decide to get one night's rest before heading back to shore. At night, you lie upon the beach, staring into the clear night sky, just quietly pondering. Then suddenly, the whole beach lights up with a brilliant and intense white light, whose source you cannot determine. There is no noise; the night is quiet and still. Yet all around you is this bright and intense white light being shone down upon you from a source above you that you cannot determine.

You look up to the sky, and you see an object that does not look familiar to you. You cannot say for sure what it is, yet your intuition tells you that it is being controlled by an intelligence that is not of this world. Henceforth, your perception of life as you previously knew and understood it has been changed forever. You know not what the source of the light was. Yet you never felt threatened or scared by its presence.

In essence, the moral of this short story is if you do not try, then you may never know. And if you do not remain open to all possibilities, then events that could have changed your life may indeed pass you by. The answers or signs that we seek are never easy to find. They remain hidden, deeply entwined in the components that make up this temporary physical reality in which we currently find ourselves. Yet if you do not trust your own instinct and undertake such journeys, then you may not find what you are looking for in this particular cycle of experience.

3

The Effects of Mass Media on the Esoteric

There has, of course, been much widespread ridicule by mainstream media (some parts, at least) in relation to all things spiritual, although the signs are that this is starting to get better and that things are changing. Indeed, it seems that in some sections of the aforementioned media, religion is an accepted train of thought (and rightly so for obvious reasons), yet when you mention spirituality, some people think that perhaps you have turned into someone different, for reasons that they may not necessarily be able to describe or articulate in a manner that makes sense to even themselves.

Stereotypical connotations instantly pop into the minds of some, based upon only what they have read rather than what they have experienced. Again, this is not necessarily a good or bad thing, but rather perhaps it is suggestive more of a state of understanding that is based only upon a rather narrow perspective. Spirituality cannot be defined according to one's appearance or mannerisms; it is far too broad and too complex to be put into a metaphorical box.

The truth is if you are reading this, then you are alive. You are a living force of energy about which so little is actually known. Therefore, you have within you this force of energy that cannot always be described with any great sense of detailed and universal accuracy. It can, of course, be felt but not defined. Such definition cannot be currently cited by science, medicine, or indeed stories of creation that have been handed down from generation to generation and that have, in some cases, been altered or twisted to service the interests of those who desire control at the cost of spiritual freedom.

Yet from the billions of bytes of information that surround us and that are told to and impressed upon us by others (sometimes forcibly), we are able to and still can piece together certain parts of the jigsaw that can indeed help to broaden our own understanding and knowledge.

We feel the presence of an inner energy, and yet we tend to often just accept it as if it were something we live with rather than live according to. Some parts of society have taught many souls not to question the origins of the powerful energy that we feel within us and that leaves our physical shells when the time comes for us to depart this sphere of experience.

Even the most hardened sceptics of all things spiritual and esoteric cannot deny that there is something to our presence in the here and now that speaks to our inner curiosity, that feeling of "There must be more to life than this" or "What is the reason for us being here?"

Maybe some souls desire to attribute our being and presence here to the doctrines contained within various religions. Of course, that is fine. Yet in the twelve months since forming the Council of Enlightened, I have noted that many souls have found that although religion did not necessarily provide them with all the answers that they were looking for, it did indeed initiate their sense of desire for further understanding and for additional information.

But on many occasions and in many instances, there was an event of emotional uncoupling from various systems of belief that needed to be transited through before one could venture out into the largely unexplored world of the unseen and the unheard. Of course, such an event of uncoupling or disassociation does not mean that one need forget that which one has been taught in relation to the brave and pioneering souls that have been before us.

The truth (according to my own perspective and understanding), as is mentioned in our YouTube introduction video, which can be found on our main site (www.councilofenlightened.org), is that you are able to keep in your perspective all that you believe in relation to your religion, and yet still venture further inward for a greater sense of a more enlightened understanding as to the origin of everything that piques your curiosity.

Fear, whether rational or not, of the unknown has so often been the stop sign in relation to undergoing or undertaking a voyage of inner self-discovery. Fear that you might be ridiculed by your friends and family. Fear that you will be ostracized by your work colleagues. Fear that your boss may think that you need a time-out. However, to be fearful is to hold a state of mind that shies away from the faith that we have in the guiding source of pure love, from which we should not expect or demand anything in return. Rather, by embracing love, we can permeate love. It is my understanding and belief—again, according to my own perspective—that there is no greater energy than that of pure love.

Although when we turn on the mainstream news channels, it can seem as though love, and its effects on this world in the sense that we understand them, can sometimes be in very short supply, love is nonetheless always there, even when we think that it has left us or, indeed, we it. One can only imagine how our world would be, and the discoveries that would be made, if we loved others, even those with whom we disagree on subjects that are very close to our hearts, as we (should) love ourselves, our children, or our pets. It's easy to imagine, if you try…

Even those obsessed with power and money could still exist quite contently in a world that is motivated by love. Why? Because the soul yearns for understanding via a myriad of different experiences. Some of these experiences may indeed be negative in their effects. For example, if you currently work for someone who comes under the aforementioned category, then such a negative environment may indeed lead you to seek out positive experiences that you may not have otherwise done were it not for the negative work environment in which you may be.

But as you start to venture forward on your journey or to progress with your inner understanding, your journey toward your own self-enlightenment will eventually show that love with all its true and pure glory can be found within all that is, because love is all there is.

When I refer to love, I do not necessarily refer to material acts of love, such as buying your girlfriend that expensive diamond ring. Nor do

I necessarily mean buying your boyfriend that gift experience of driving that supercar around a race track. By referring to love, I am referring to that pure, divine, and often subliminal energy that finds itself deep within your soul. We can all sense it, perhaps just in different ways because maybe, as with the spirit, love cannot be defined; rather, it is something that can only be felt.

Yet when you look at your children, your pets, or your partner in the eye and there is a sense of energy that manifests into your physical body, by perhaps giving you goosebumps or by sending shivers down and up your spine, then this is what I mean by sensing and feeling pure love. Or maybe when you stare out into a starlit sky, to be met only with the sheer beauty of the cosmos, which then has the effect and feeling of energizing your entire body. Ultimately, love has many forms, but its sense of fulfillment and oneness can be shared by all, and it can also be accessed by all.

Finding true and pure love can act as the catalyst and start of your own journey toward self-discovery. Tuning into that which makes everything tick can start a chain reaction on your path that leads to a sense of true purpose and discovery, especially if you are able to still hold on to love in the face of negative encounters.

By holding pure love in your heart, you may indeed find balance. By also purging all feelings that are generated by, for example, fear, you may find that only the feeling and notion of love will fill the void that is left after letting go of things such as fear. It is always tempting, when discussing fear, to cover subjects that are the cause of such feelings, such as death.

However, it is my understanding that one cannot talk effectively about such things via a medium as public as a book, because in order to truly discuss subjects as complicated as death, one must first understand where the current perception of the audience or the listener actually is.

And of course, this is not entirely possible via a one-way communicational exchange such as a book. Yet within the council itself, we do have various mediums for discussing such topics, but they are currently all online.

4

What Is the Purpose of the Council?

The Council of Enlightened was formed based on a very deep and genuine desire to bring together those among us who are becoming increasingly aware that there is indeed more to our physical reality than what simply meets the physical eye or our physical senses, and that there is more to this particular reality than what is often accepted by the mainstream media outlets.

Each of us has at some point, I am sure, pondered the meaning of this life and indeed the reason for our being here. Although it seems unlikely that there is a single generic and easily definable reason for us being here, there certainly seems to be some common factors and principles that indicate some of the potential reasons behind our being here, in this particular time and place.

Our present ability to experience events, circumstances, and emotions within this realm in a material and physical sense, via the myriad of different catalysts or synchronicities and experiences that lie before us, can indeed help us to understand more about the age-old question: Why are we here? But ultimately, one must seek the answer within by one's own journey.

My own such journey toward this sense of understanding started some twenty-three years ago. Of course, it has not ended, as I am still very much learning. Maybe over time, my questions have changed, as those questions that I asked over two decades ago I feel, at least, have to some extent been answered. But as is often the case, one answered question often leads to more curiosity and a deeper desire for even further and more detailed understanding.

Going back to what started my own journey, and thus led to the formation of the Council of Enlightened, when I was thirteen years of age, I remember, while lying in bed on a clear and quiet night, staring at the pristine and radiant moon through the open doors that were adjacent to the small balcony outside of my room and thinking about the meaning behind all that we currently see, hear, and feel. In essence, I pondered the wonders of creation, as we all often do.

I think I asked this question at such an early age because of what was going on in my life at the time. I was not happy and was trying to understand why we are here, when here can sometimes be so utterly depressing and negative.

As soon as I pondered this question quietly within my own frame of conscience, I had a very profound feeling and a very strong sense that I was not ready to know the answer (according to my own perceptions). I cannot tell you where this feeling came from, just that it was a very real and almost-tangible thought process that entered my mind immediately after thinking about the question in a very sincere and curious manner.

I did not sense that there was no answer, just that the answer can only truly be appreciated, comprehended, and understood by having undertaken a lengthy, arduous, and eventful journey of exploring our own selves and the environment in which we find ourselves at this present moment in time, as we currently measure it. Thereto started a journey that has thus far lasted over two decades and has, to date, led to the formation of the Council of Enlightened, for reasons that I must admit that I do not yet fully understand.

During my journey so far, I have had many experiences, both extremely positive and extremely negative. I have witnessed and directly experienced many things that modern, current-day science cannot always explain. Indeed, many of these experiences occurred while I was serving in my country's armed forces and then its emergency services for a combined total of over fifteen years.

The unexplainable experiences of which I speak were varied, and I never felt threatened or scared in the traditional sense before, during, or after these experiences. But looking back now, I have a very sincere feeling that the experiences all had their own messages contained within them. I would not say that I understood all of the events or that I was able to decipher the potential lessons to be learned from them, but I do get a deep sense and understanding as to why they occurred and when they happened as they did.

I shall not spend too much time talking about my own experiences in this book, because this is really about the Council of Enlightened, and more importantly you (or rather, your soul) and how your soul can indeed connect to its path for which it came here to potentially fulfill.

Needless to say, however, that about twelve months ago (June 2015), I genuinely believe that I finally pieced together the many pieces to the incredibly complex jigsaw (according to my own understanding and perception), and I believe that I found an answer, or perhaps maybe I was led to such an answer to the question that I had pondered so many years ago. Or at the very least, an answer that resonates with my own perception.

Of course, I could be wrong. But then, I only ever believe that which my instinct informs me to be true, and I have entrusted such a feeling previously with my own life. With so many messages, whether on TV, online, or just about anywhere else that you can think of, I very much believe that one should always listen to one's own instinct in order to be informed of what one should and should not accept as being one's own truths.

Not too long after this extended chapter in my life (the chapter of experience in order to gain a deeper sense of understanding), I felt a very strong inclination within my conscience that I should form the Council of Enlightened so that other like-minded awoken souls could come together with the aim of finding their own truths. Not to have my or others' truths dictated to them, but rather to seek solace and comfort in the company of other like-minded souls.

I feel that it is important to point out at this stage that it is not my aim or intention to try to impress upon others that which I have come to understand about this temporary reality. Rather, I feel passionately about helping others to find the answers to their own questions, whatever they may be. It is this process of finding answers to questions that motivates me, rather than the questions and the answers themselves.

The sense of purpose that I felt in relation to the inception of the Council of Enlightened was not organic in its form and origin. That is to say, the thought patterns and impressions behind the rationale that led to the formation of the council did not seem to originate from my own soul's innate thinking. Where these thoughts came from, I do not exactly know. Maybe one day, I shall find out. It matters not, at this moment, as to the source behind such thoughts although I am truly grateful for their presence in my conscious mind.

Those who have suddenly had thoughts pop into their minds that were completely unrelated to what they may have been thinking about at the time before such thoughts entered their minds will be able to relate to what I am attempting to describe. It is almost as if a subtle train of thought has been very discreetly placed into one's mind.

At the same time (immediately prior to the inception of the Council of Enlightened), there was also a very high volume of synchronicities that were finding their way into my particular timeline. But again, the details regarding these synchronicities, and the effect that they had on my own conscience, are not really for this book, as this book is about helping others to find their own truths.

Of course, and as mentioned earlier, no one within the council claims to be 100 percent enlightened, for I do not believe that one can really ever be fully 100 percent enlightened to all there ever was, is, and will be—at least not within this lifetime while located in this particular realm. Rather, all council members assert that they are aware of their own paths toward their own self-enlightenment. They may not know where their paths may take them, just that there is a unique path toward which they walk with an open mind and open heart.

So in summary, I guess you could say that the Council of Enlightened is here to allow individuals the ability to share thoughts, experiences, perspectives, and feelings about this reality in an open and engaging forum. This forum and information exchange enables much to be pondered and to be considered that perhaps would have otherwise not been considered.

Eventually, the case may be that those who participate within the forum that the Council of Enlightened has created may in some way become enlightened to their own senses of purpose and their own senses of deep understanding about the temporary reality in which we currently find ourselves.

5

Self-Enlightenment

But what is, or rather how could we perhaps define the term, "self-enlightenment"? Think maybe of self-enlightenment as being able to understand why you are here on this particular journey and what the environment around you, according to your own perspective, means to you and that journey. Think also of self-enlightenment as being the realization of who and what you really are.

As a rather simplistic example, imagine that you are driving along a road through the middle of your nearest city with several family members or friends in the same car. As you drive through the streets, each person in the car looks out of his or her window and sees things that perhaps the others may not, yet they are all in the same car, on the same street, at the same time, and at the same moment. What they see relative to their shared journey and what they look at will depend upon their individual perspectives in relation to where in the car they are sitting and which direction they look in, often depending on what piques each individual's curiosity.

Self-enlightenment could also be seen as being the degree of understanding in relation to your own perception of that which surrounds you, both in terms of what can be seen and in terms of what cannot be seen. It could indeed also be the ability to determine what the experiences that lie before you may mean for your path, and also the ability to extract from these experiences a deeper understanding about your environment.

JJJ

It is my understanding that no two life experiences are really ever exactly the same. Of course, there are some common and fundamental physical characteristics about this realm and the experiences that occur within it that we can all relate to, but the manner in which we interact with such physical characteristics will be unique according to our own perspectives. Our local star, the sun, is one such example of something that we can sense but that has different meaning to different people. We each feel its presence in one way or another. Whether by sight, by feel, or by some other sense, it is hard not to notice our sun, either directly or indirectly.

Yet we each have a different and unique experience with this body of energy that we have collectively called the sun. For some, it can cause physical pain; for others, it can bring physical pleasure. Realizing, in this example, what role the sun can have during your own life journey is just one part of the bigger picture of understanding your own journey to be had here: being enlightened to the journey of self while understanding that you still constitute a vital element of the whole, or perhaps of everything.

Grasping the concept and notion of self-enlightenment may sound like pure fiction. Many people have become accustomed to the notion that there is perhaps no real meaning behind life. They believe everything is just an amazing collaboration of something that not even the most intelligent mind currently on earth can create. We, as a whole, tend not to understand how we actually got here. It is a question that remains largely unanswered. So often it's easier just to accept that we are here because, well, just because. Yet to many of you, something does not stack up with this slumber-derived rationale of mere coincidence. You sense that there is indeed a much deeper understanding to be found. You may not know where this understanding comes from, but you feel its gentle pull on your own curiosity and conscience.

But self-enlightenment is a real notion and state of understanding that deserves much more thought time and much more effort. Why try to figure out everyone else's truth before coming to terms with your own? Surely we must first gain an understanding as to what our own paths mean for us, and would it not make sense to try to realign with our inner selves before trying to adopt other people's understandings and perceptions as our own if indeed such practices are appropriate to our own timelines?

Gaining this insight of self-enlightenment can change the course of your path here and point you ultimately to a destination that perhaps you never even knew existed or perhaps one that you had previously not even considered. You may think currently that your only purpose in life is to work, socialize, get married, have children, and then retire. And of course, there is nothing wrong with this whatsoever. Yet ponder first the notion that something may indeed be missing, and then perhaps consider how you can indeed find this missing piece of your own puzzle.

Of course, we can always look to others in relation to guidance and direction. But perhaps more importantly, one should always try to listen to one's own guidance and inner direction, while always taking into account external influences such as the guidance of others. It cannot be ignored that there are indeed many souls currently here who have teachings and knowledge of great importance and significance. Yet always your inner self will give you a gentle nudge in the right direction for as long as you are connected to your inner, and indeed higher, self.

There are many methods and teachings that can help your soul to reconnect with its intended path and thus give understanding to your reason or reasons for being here, in this time and in this place. There are far too many modalities and methods to list within the scope of this book. A good place to start, however, is with simple, harmonic, and pure contemplation and meditation. Meditation can help bring light to the doorway of your own path to discovery, while you are always being mindful of factors that may act to sway you from such a path.

Factors, influences, and experiences that can have the effect of swaying your soul from its own path could include, for example, the influence of others around you who may be perfectly happy staying in the cyclical state of slumber. Of course, it is not for us to judge such states of mind or those who adopt them. Rather, those of us who wish to continue with the journey of self-discovery can simply allow such influences to wash over our own senses of reasoning and understanding. We can allow the thoughts and emotional influences of others to enter and then exit the residence within our physical bodies of the soul. Of course, such discipline takes much time and practice and requires the soul to try to maintain a sense of delicate balance, yet not allowing the opinions, perceptions, and thoughts of others to adversely affect our own balances can indeed be ultimately achieved.

Of course, it is also natural for one to deviate, from time to time, from that which one feels one is familiar with. Such a process of deviation and exploration can enrich the dynamic flow of experience and catalyst. I am always mindful when those joining the council enter the organization to ensure that new members reflect on the notion that no soul should overtly try to pull someone away from his or her own path. If shared perspectives help to open new doors of discovery, then great. Yet such doors must be open according to the free will of those seeking such doors.

Control does not seem conducive to the divine harmony and importance of free will. For example, your neighbor's truths will not necessarily be the same as yours, yet this does not mean that your neighbor's truths are any less real or are any less important or significant. We can still learn a great deal from those who have different journeys to undertake from our own. Being open to all teachings, all wisdom, and all knowledge is such a vital part of each step along your journey, and it is these steps of infinite experience about which we share information within the council.

Can you just imagine how much negative emotion would be dissipated if everyone started a sentence, when talking about his or her beliefs, by stating "it is my understanding" or "according to my own perceptions" (touched on again further on in this book)? I am fairly confident that such words would indeed negate the need for anyone privy to hearing such thoughts and feelings that do not resonate with his or her own thoughts and feelings to adopt a defensive state or mind.

Ultimately, we have all probably come from a place that cannot be fully described but instead only felt. We have all come here for individual reasons, experiences, and lessons. To try to affix one universal overlay to all such infinite reasons and rationales is folly. In order for us to evolve, let us leave behind the old ways and mechanisms of thinking. The universe is indeed keen to show us what else there is to discover in this reality.

But we must first learn to connect to that which we all feel, and we must learn to be guided by our own instincts and accept that each soul has its own path to walk before the universe accepts us onto its truly wondrous and magnificent stage. To work toward enlightenment, we must first navigate the hurdle and teachings of self-enlightenment. I feel sincerely that the more who become aware of such self-enlightenment, then the quicker this civilization will ascend into the planes of higher truths and realization.

Why do I sense and feel this? Well, I guess you could say that it is just a feeling that I have and have always had. And of course, I am not alone in this sense and with this feeling. Many, many souls feel the tide of change is underway albeit in the background. Yet behind the scenes, there takes place a gentle sway of influence in order to try to prevent this civilization, in this moment of time, from making the mistakes of past civilizations that were once incarnate upon this sphere that we call Earth.

Will this gentle sway and influence make a difference and prevent us from making mistakes that lead to the demise of that with which we are currently familiar? Only time will tell, as it is measured in this reality. Yet each soul currently present has an important role and part to play in the shaping of our immediate and distant physical future.

6

Synchronicities

When I refer to synchronicities, I refer to often what may seem like random events or incidents occurring and happening in the material or physical world that seem to reinforce a notion or vision that you have or have had within the realms of your own conscience. Often, you are able to identify the difference between a random event and a synchronicity, as your instinct will highlight to you the event in question.

It is almost as if what seems on its face to be a random event is not so random. You seem to be able to sense that the event in question has happened for a reason or reasons that only your own conscience would seem to understand and make sense of.

For example, when perhaps reading a random newspaper or news website or maybe even when scanning the Internet looking for a new job, you see a job advert that resonates deeply with a childhood ambition that you perhaps once had but had forgotten about—maybe because the everyday trials and tribulations of life have gotten in the way. Yet also, the paper or website you are reading is not one you would usually pick up or visit.

However, following your instinctive feeling, you apply for the job on a whim and end up, following a successful interview, getting it. In this new job, imagine that you meet another soul with whom you instantly connect. It is as if you have known each other for an eternity. Following a whirlwind romance, you end up settling down and starting a family with what feels like your soul mate. Imagine that all of this took place within the space of just a few months and that immediately before responding to that job interview, you had been quietly pondering how fed up you were with, in this example, being single.

Of course, some people may say that such an event was merely just a coincidence, that it was a random encounter that statistically should or could happen to anyone anytime. Of course, that would indeed be their own opinions, to which they are entitled as it is a fundamental principle of their own perceptions of your events. And of course, as we have already mentioned, such a perception is unique to the individual soul witnessing the event, based upon the many, many experiences that it is to have and has already had within this realm.

And let us not forget that no other person will know the same feelings that you have in relation to such an incident and the circumstances surrounding it, if it were indeed to occur. And it is this feeling that informs your own conscience as to the origin and form of such an event. Was it a coincidence, or was it indeed an event that was destined to happen to you while you were here? The truth is, only you will know the answer to this question.

I am not saying or suggesting here that every event happens based on the same rationale as outlined above. The key is in trying to differentiate between random events and events that have occurred on your own path for reasons to do with your own purpose for being here. There are many, many different methods for trying to differentiate between the random events and the events that have indeed occurred for good reason—far too many methods to discuss in this book. However, when trying to ascertain whether something has happened for a specific reason, try maybe just to ponder the event and the feelings that it gave you, and then just let the thought go and see what comes back from the ether of the infinite. It may take an hour, a day, a month, a year, or even a decade. But eventually, the answer shall find you, just as long as you remain open to receiving it.

Of course, when discussing such things as the meaning behind events that are personal to you, it matters not what others think according to their own unique perceptions. If you are aware or remain open to all possibilities, and you encounter some event that you think is a synchronicity, and your instinct tells you that it is just that, then, well, it is. There are no right or wrong answers, merely information that may or may not resonate with your soul according to your own unique perception. The gentle pull from within of that which we cannot always describe but that many refer to as the higher self is what will ultimately inform you as to what is and is not relevant to your own path.

That is not to say that if you are not aware or you are not open to such possibilities, then you do not have synchronicities, for I believe that such things are universally applicable to all souls regardless of their sense of understanding. However, by being aware and open, you have a much greater and significant chance of not only detecting and identifying the synchronicity before you but also being able to decipher what it means for your own soul and your own path during this particular cycle of experience, or life, to use its more common reference.

I should perhaps also point out that I do believe that we each have the ability to become aware but that such a process is not an easy or straightforward one. As with much in this cycle of life, there are many obstacles to overcome before one becomes truly aware and thus 100 percent open to all that surrounds our physical and emotional senses. However, it is indeed a journey well worth embarking upon. Gaining a deep sense of spiritual awareness can dramatically change your life.

Again, such a topic is not really for this book, as it deserves specific attention. But as is always the case, your inner self can indeed shine light on the answers to such questions.

7

Making the Connection

Part of the process of understanding that accompanies finding the true purpose behind your own journey here comes with being able to distinguish your own organic thoughts, those bits and pieces of information that have found their way into your conscience naturally, from those thoughts that originate from a source that is external to the aforementioned.

I refer to thoughts and visions that typically come into your conscience when meditating, when contemplating, or at times of deep relaxation rather than those thoughts that come to you when contemplating the more mundane components of this physical reality. Those of you reading this who meditate often will perhaps know exactly what I mean. In essence, when you clear the field of your conscious vision, the thoughts and images that then enter such a place (your conscience) are what I am referring to.

Our consciences are constantly bombarded with a huge amount and vast array of information, both from the physical environment in which we currently find ourselves and from an environment that is beyond the scope of this book to describe in any great detail, but let us call it the ether.

Information from the ether can find its way into our own thought patterns, whether directly or indirectly. This information can sometimes be at odds with what we believe or with what we feel or have perhaps been taught by others. However, one particular source of information and guidance that will not let you down is your instinct or your higher self.

Your instinct is the source of information within your soul that allows you to discern information that is relevant to your path from information that is perhaps not directly relevant (for example, deciding on which flavor drink to buy versus where to live). The key to deciphering this flow of intricate and detailed information is being able first to find it and then to listen to it and, according to your own free will, act upon such information as and when you see fit.

Learning to listen to the true voice of your instinct is not an easy or quick process. However, it never really was meant to be; otherwise, the experiences that we came here for would not carry with them the same rich influence that they currently do. It takes time, dedication, patience, and much practice to be able to cancel out the background noise and influences created by the materialistic part of society and to listen instead to your own guidance and instinctive rationale.

There are many methods that can speed up or assist with this process, just as there are many distractions that can sway you away from such an ability and aim. Part of the process of experience (both current and former) is to refine these practices so that you can indeed become more in tune with your own sources of reasoning and rationale, which have been shaped over (perhaps) many previous incarnate experiences.

However, once found and once tuned fully into, the guidance of your instinct will not let your soul down for as long as your soul and conscience remain in good balance and surrounded by pure and divine love. I won't define love in the sense that I understand it, as love means different things to different souls. What is important is to embrace the true harmonic field and energy associated with love, whether it's being in love or having love for something.

Your instinct will allow you to be able to make not necessarily the right or wrong decisions about factors that affect your life, but it will allow you to make decisions that are relevant to your own path. The reason behind the events that lie before you and that have already been before you, leading to the experiences that you have had and will have.

Some of these experiences may not make sense. They may make you feel extremely sad or make you feel negative. They may even lead you to have thoughts about ending your current cycle of experience. If this happens, push on. Carry on with your inward journey. Do not give up, and do not give up on hope, for it shall never give up on you. Indeed, I believe that thoughts associated with the desire to end your cycle of experience early may mean that you are closer to finding that connection than what you may think.

Why? Well, to feel a sense of desire to return back to that place from where we came means that perhaps indeed you have started to reconnect with such a place without even being consciously aware of such. After all, if you feel like returning back, then this means that you may have considered the notion that there is indeed somewhere rather than simply nowhere.

I do talk from personal experience here. A few years ago, I was on the verge of losing my business, having been seriously let down by individuals whom, at the time, I thought that I could trust. I had already had quite a few intense experiences along my journey during my childhood, during the time that I spent in the armed forces, and during the time that I spent in the emergency services of the country in which I am currently domicile.

At the time in question, I remember sitting at my local train station and thinking about just bringing it all to an end—but then I thought that if indeed I was willing to call it a day, so to speak, then I could also face the challenges that lay before me. It also made me realize that my soul was yearning to return…but return to what exactly? This question alone made me want to venture further into the realms of the unknown—and that is exactly what happened and is still taking place to this day.

During the work that I do with the Council of Enlightened, I speak with many people. I am truly honored that they trust me, so they are happy to share some very intimate experiences and thoughts with me. Many such experiences relate to coping with feelings of ending their current cycles of experience. So if you have had or do have these thoughts, then you are not alone. But don't give up on yourself. In the illusion of this reality, it is easy to get lost in the maze of depression that, at some point, visits us all.

8

The Soul's Balance

Above, I mentioned about how important I felt it was to try to balance the energy and polarity of your soul. Let me expand upon what I mean by this statement: It is my understanding and perception of the underlying dynamic of the soul that when we arrive here, so to speak, our souls find themselves in the equilibrium of a fine balance.

That is to say, they are neither polarized overtly toward the positive or overtly toward the negative. Indeed, the soul may contain some element of predefined purpose according to that which we have come here to experience, but I believe that as an energy form, at least, our souls resonate according to the initial balance of neutrality.

It is the experiences that are to come that mold the energetic sphere of the soul toward the polarity that, for example, it currently finds itself in. And of course, it is indeed possible to change such polarity according to the desires of your own free will.

I shall not try to define negative and positive here, as such a definition depends entirely on the perspective of the soul. It is never wise to try to define something that has no singular definition in relation to that which it refers to, in a descriptive sense at least.

As our souls experience childhood and its many, many lessons, they are subject to many different forms of quite often very profound and significant energies. Some of these experiences are, of course, positive. Some are negative, and some are neutral. I feel personally that the challenge comes in trying to afford our souls, after physical adolescence, the same balance that they had when they first entered this domain here on this particular sphere that we refer to as Earth.

Trying to rebalance the soul is not an easy task. It takes much time and patience and requires being open to the catalysts and synchronicities that come your way. Yet for as long as you are able to sustain the energies associated with hope, love, peace, and harmony, then indeed, anything is possible, according to the parameters that have been laid out within this physical reality.

But what are the positive reasons for trying to reach and maintain that balance? How does having a positive balance assist you as you navigate through your journey on this trip we call life?

I feel that it is important at this stage to point out that one should never shy away from or back away from allowing the experience that comes with the catalytic event before you to reach your soul, and thus, by doing so (backing away), potentially inhibit the experience or lesson for which the event was intended.

For according to my own understanding and according to my own perception, the experience or lesson to be had from the catalytic event that was missed shall keep reappearing on your soul's timeline, whether in this life or perhaps the next. The circumstances may be different, yet the potential affect could be more or less the same.

As an example, let us assume there is a nonspecific event before you, which can be anything, that has the purpose and intent of highlighting to you that there is someone in your current and present life who can help open, broaden, and widen your perspective and latent awareness. Let us assume for a moment that you miss the event in question. I believe that events shall keep occurring before you, gently guiding your soul in the direction of the individual who can assist you, until such time as the connection is made according to the desires of your own free will.

Of course, as always, the reoccurrence of the event can depend upon what your soul set out to achieve before it incarnated into this particular timeline, the experiences for which it came here for. Only your own soul can truly and genuinely inform you as to what it is that you have come here for. And of course, there are souls also present within our current collective timeline who can help you to reconnect to your inner self, and in doing so thus help your soul to read the signals and catalytic events that find their harmonic chord and subsequent resonance within your soul's conscience.

By achieving and maintaining the soul's balance, you are able to undertake the experience of the catalytic event that lies before you, and yet the event may not adversely alter the divine energetic balance of your soul. With the soul in fine balance, we can experience the various experiences, observe them, learn from them, gain greater understanding from them, yet not let them permanently sway or alter the configuration of the soul as it was when it entered this particular experience of incarnation.

It is as if we almost observe and witness the experience, but we do not let the experience affect the divinity and balance of the soul. Picture and visualize a certain element of detachment from your physical surroundings (while still remaining grounded), yet keep yourself harmonized so as to not detach too much from the physicality of your local reality.

The effect of becoming too detached and thus drifting into the realms where the soul feels the gentle and subtle pull is almost like when a butterfly gets carried away off course on a gentle wind, while still fluttering its wings in order to try to get to a destination that it does not necessarily understand or fully comprehend. This is why it is important to remain grounded and not become too detached from your direct environment.

Of course, during our life cycles here, we are inevitably and almost certainly going to be occasionally pulled in one direction and off course (relatively speaking) toward the positive or the negative energy. The period during which we find ourselves aligned to negative or positive polarity may last a day, a week, a month, a decade, or even maybe a lifetime (during this cycle of experience). Yet according to my own perception and understanding, the soul will always strive to try to get back to its balanced state, having still learned from the uncountable and undefinable experiences that we are to have while here but at the same time not allowing such experiences to alter the divine dynamic of the soul.

I feel that at this stage, it is important to note that keeping one's physical vessel, or body, healthy is a vital tool in assisting the soul to find its balance. Just as we would not expect our cars to take us on a long journey if we did not maintain them well, how can we expect our bodies to carry our souls to their destinations here if we do not eat healthily, exercise, and generally take care of our physical vessels?

Cleansing one's vessel and keeping it as pure as possible can have a profound effect on the soul and its journey. The bond between your soul and your body is so very powerful. Yet it is only temporary. Your body deserves to be nourished with that which it needs in order to maintain its delicate function. I am not advocating a particular diet or means by which I think others should live; such decisions must be made by the individual. Yet when you find yourself alone in a quiet place, with no distractions, simply try to listen to the energy of your own body. Tune into its physical structure, just as the soul can tune into any physical and immaterial energy. You may be surprised as to what you sense, feel, and hear.

Consider and ponder also that the soul can perhaps become overpolarized toward one particular energy. Ponder that the soul can become entangled with all the information that it tries to decipher and understand. As an example of this, of the many thousands of e-mails and messages that I get from souls enquiring about joining the council, there seems to be a common extreme event that has immediately preceded their newfound awareness. Often, this event is profoundly negative in nature, yet often it leads to something that is extremely positive: the sense or reconnection to that energy that we feel deep within our souls, the ever-present feeling of knowing.

Therefore, it is vital to undertake a regular and routine process of indexing the information or events that occur before you so that your soul can perhaps make sense of them all (the experience) and their intended purposes. The manner and technique in which this indexing can be achieved may vary according to your physical self and what helps to relax your mind, body, and spirit. It may be meditation or yoga or perhaps regular exercise, or indeed a combination of the three, or perhaps even the exchange of physical energy with another consenting soul. Whatever the method, I feel that it is important to ensure that your soul takes some time to truly switch off and go within so that it can effectively regroup and reconnect with all that makes you, well, you.

This extreme period of negative polarity that may lead to your subsequent awareness or awakening can indeed be a very sensitive and extremely important time period for your soul. For if you do not recover your balance after such an event, then you could spend the rest of your life during this cycle of experience with a soul that cannot regain its central balance and thus fails to navigate the maze before it. It is almost as if the soul is caught in a whirlpool or vortex of extreme emotions and feelings that came as a result of, or occurred immediately before, the extreme catalytic event happened.

It may be that emotions such as regret, jealously, hate, fear, or self-pity create the kind of negative energy vortex that the energy of the soul gets caught up in and cannot easily escape. That is not to say that escape from the negative vortex is not possible, just that it may take some time, some patience, some perseverance, and indeed some external or outside help. Of course we all have, at some point or other, whether in this life or perhaps a previous one, fallen into a negative vortex; such a process is an important and often fundamental catalyst for the further understanding and awareness of the soul.

At the time, the negative vortex may not make sense. It may lead your soul's conscience to think that there really is no way out of this negative vortex of extreme emotion. Yet there is and always will be a way. During this time, one of the most important things to keep in your perspective is the energy associated with the feeling and sense of hope, and never give up on it.

In fact, assisting in regrouping or rebalancing the soul's energy is one of the many reasons as to why the council has been formed: so that souls can come together, regardless of background or experience, in order to share the positive energy of pure love with one another and to help the soul regain its vital balance so that it can continue forward on its journey.

The council itself cares not for race, sex, wealth, political affiliation, views, or background. It focuses on only that common and fundamental divine energy that we each share: the soul.

Personally, I feel that inner guidance, shared knowledge (through experience and catalyst), and understanding are some of the most important traits to possess while we are here. Of course, some events defy explanation and leave the observer of such events feeling that there cannot be any good on his or her and others' timelines because of, or attributable to, such events. It is not for me to try to make sense of such events, because in truth it is down to our own individual perceptions to try to gain the understanding and meaning behind all that occurs, whether positive, negative, or neutral. And, of course, there is and will always be a meaning in some manner or another. One just has to try to find it.

Yet there seems to be a mysterious principle at work behind the scenes that appears inextricably connected and linked to all that occurs within this particular physical reality, in both the positive and the negative. It is this common principle that I have spent the last twenty-three years trying to understand and learn more about. Of course, I am sure there are many, many varying principles at work, each one playing a significant part in the intricate workings of this delicate reality. I think that we each have our own gentle pulls toward whichever principle allows us to learn more about our individual reasons for being here. Your own free will, I am sure, will guide you to yours.

But ultimately, maintaining an inner balance can help you to navigate the path before you and prepare you for what it may have in store. It is entirely normal to experience adjustments in this balance from time to time. Yet being able to revert back to the state of balance can help you also to not become unduly displaced, in an energetic form, from your surroundings and environment

9

Perception and Understanding

When considering and contemplating the balance of your own soul and the energy associated with it, perhaps consider that it matters not whether your perception or understanding is not the same perception or understanding that is accepted or understood by those souls around you. Our perceptions and understandings do not have to align completely in order for harmony to ensue. I am always at a loss when trying to make sense of the rationale behind different souls trying to convince other souls that their own truths should be adopted by others who might be on a completely different path from their own.

Fear no doubt plays a significant part in this. Fear that just because someone else's reality differs from your own, then such a different perspective means that your own observations are any less valid. One need only consider the notion of the multiverse in order to realize that perhaps there is no single universal overlay of reality that applies to all.

Consider and ponder that the billions of souls that share this time and place with us are all having their own unique experiences as guided by their own intuitions, influenced both internally and externally. Therefore, if something that you understand to be your own truth does not resonate with another soul's truth, then it matters not. Such a difference in perspective does not mean that your own views are any less valid or are untrue. Because really, there are limitless truths and possibilities. Society has just been hoodwinked into thinking that there is a blanket truth that should be accepted, applied, and adhered to by all, when this is perhaps really not the case.

Even if we perhaps preceded each observation and subsequent perception with the words "according to my own perception" or "it is my own understanding, based upon what I have experienced," then we would certainly find that the words that came after such a statement would reach listeners without their instinctively feeling that they must defend their own truths. As another albeit similar example, but this time using different components to such an example, let us assume that we swam in the same lake located in the same part of the county, but that I spent most of my time swimming underwater, while you spent most of your time above or on the water.

If I said to you, upon reaching the other side, "The water is dark green" (because, let's assume, at a certain depth it is), but you, seeing only the blue shade of the water on the surface, affirmed, "Absolutely not, the water is blue," then no doubt an argument or heated conversation may then ensue. However, if I said, "According to my own perception, the water was dark green," then you would instantly understand that I am merely relaying that which I have experienced rather than trying to convince you that the water is green, when in truth, we were swimming in the same place but just had different experiences relative to our surroundings while in that same place.

It would be interesting to see what effect this simple statement would have in situations where subjects are being discussed that often lead to heated arguments and debates. I think that perhaps, while still being energetic, such discussions would not lead to the type of outcome that often accompanies such emotionally charged subjects.

To bring together open-minded souls who are truly advancing on their own paths of self-discovery and self-enlightenment means that fellow souls can interact with much more enrichment in relation to the knowledge that is being shared, based on the understanding that just as there are an infinite number of realities, so too are there an infinite number of experiences and possible truths. There is no single truth that is applicable to all within the realms of this particular arena of experience that we call life. Of course, there are some fundamental, universally applicable forces and energies that regulate the physical dynamic of the arena in which we currently find ourselves, such as the beautiful and divine energy of love. Yet even with love, the manifestations of such are extremely varied, numerous, and, ultimately, infinite.

Thus, by accepting or perhaps even just pondering that we are not in a collective competition of fundamental truths, and that there can be potentially many, many truths, we open our fields of innate perception and acceptance further still to the infinite amount of potential truths and perceptions that exist beyond the realm and confines of time, as we experience and measure such, in this particular cycle of understanding.

With these thoughts in mind, we can open ourselves to not only trains of thought that resonate within our souls, as per our own understandings, but also to trains of thought that, although they may not resonate with our own understandings in this moment of time, could indeed lead to new experiences and catalysts that open new perspectives and fields of view in the future and also in the now.

And with these new perceptions and fields of view, you may find that right in front of you, all along, were hidden truths relative to your own path that make so much sense to you but that you may have previously discredited. Perhaps once you find these new perceptions, then you will be left perplexed as to how you ever interpreted the world around you without such perceptions and fields of view.

In essence, to complete the jigsaw puzzle, we must look at all the pieces from many different angles and perspectives; otherwise we will just keep revisiting the same puzzle over and over again, until our perceptions change and thus we see the intricate pieces to the puzzle in orientations and configurations that we had never previously considered.

10

The Higher Conscience

Consider and perhaps ponder for a moment that your soul is linked to a reflection of itself, but that this reflection exists in a different time and in a different place from that which we experience in our current form. When I say "higher," I refer to the prospect that your higher self is currently in a domain that is very different from that in which we currently find ourselves, rather than being higher in the physical sense. So really, this higher place could be interpreted as being somewhere without the constraints that limit our current experiences in relation to the physical boundaries placed within and upon it.

So what could be the purpose of this higher conscience and ultimate reflection of you, and how do you connect to it if you so desire? Understanding the purpose of one's own individual higher self, even when considering that ultimately we are all connected as one, can only really be determined by the individual. This is because the higher conscience is unique to the individual, and so is its connection to your own soul in the here and now. The desires, aims, and purpose of your higher self can therefore only be really interpreted by your own self in the form in which it currently finds itself.

This still leaves us with the question of, if you haven't already made such a connection to your higher self, how do you connect to it? Your ability to connect to your higher self can only really occur via the exploration of various techniques that are unique and most comfortable to you. There is no one answer or method that applies to everyone. However, one such example of how you could connect to what is essentially still another part of you existing in a place much different from our current surroundings is via meditation.

Meditation can take many different forms and disciplines. For some, it may occur in a very specific set of surroundings with a specific group of people. For others, meditation may work best while undertaken or experienced alone and while listening to meditation music or various chants. For me personally, I try to maintain a meditative state at all times throughout the day. That's not to say that I walk around with my eyes closed, chanting various mantras at all times (because in today's society, the ironic thing is that doing such would probably get me sectioned, even though in some societies, such a practice is perfectly common).

Rather, I try to remain conscious of everything around me and within me at all times, and I try to keep my mind silent as often as possible so that I can sense various feelings that enter my conscience, both generated and originating from my immediate surroundings, and also generated by influences external to my immediate environment and external to my conscience (i.e., perhaps my own higher self).

It seems to me that there are more people that sense this connection to their higher selves than what you might initially think. Many people with whom I come into contact via the council refer to their higher selves in a very open manner. And of course, why shouldn't they? Some people may just dismiss their higher selves as being their imaginations, or perhaps just regular organic thought patterns from their own immediate frames of conscience. And of course, such a view is perfectly fine. As I always like to try to affirm, each individual's reality, and what it is comprised of, is unique to them.

The point of mentioning the concept of the higher self here is to plant a seed of thought for those of you who are yet to consider not only the presence of a higher self but also its implications for your own decisions so that you can explore this possibility in your own time and according to your own free will.

As an example, imagine you are faced with a decision in relation to making a choice between two different trains to board in order to get to your destination. Maybe, in this example, the train is taking you to an event that could change the course of your life. It could be to a job, or to a first date maybe. Each of the two trains before you look exactly the same; there are no distinguishing features about them whatsoever. Imagine also that they are both on the same platform and leave at the same time. They are going to the same place, arrive at the same time, and are configured exactly the same. Thus, there is nothing that differentiates the two trains, other than that they are located at slightly different locations.

Imagine that for a moment, you consider which train to get onto. You immediately ponder about which train you should jump into. Instantly, you think that train number 1 is the right one, so you start to walk toward it. However, when you are almost there, something in your head tells you to take train number 2. Most of us have had, at some point or other, this feeling that a decision that we have made might not be the right one before the outcome relative to that decision has occurred. There seems to be a very subtle push away from the course that we are currently on, relative to the decision that we have made.

Now, at this point, you may not know why, for whatever reason, train number 2 should be the right one. Yet you feel a strong sense of instinct that train number 2 is the correct one to take, so you get on it and sit down. Let's now imagine, in this scenario, that train number 1, after setting off, encounters technical problems, and thus had you stepped on it, then you would have missed your important and life-changing date or job interview. It turns out that train number 2 was indeed the right one to take in order to fulfill or set in motion a sequence of events that has the effect of changing your life.

But where or what was the source of this voice that told you, or feeling that persuaded you, to pick train number 2 as opposed to train number 1? Well, it may have just been circumstances relevant to that particular environment, such as the subtle manner in which the train you chose was bathed in sunlight at the time. Or perhaps, just maybe, it was your higher self guiding you in the direction of train number 2.

JJJ

Assume that your higher self, being a reflection of you but in a completely different place, can foresee your future timeline and the events on such a timeline. Not every exact second of it, but rather which events will enable you to fulfill the reason for your being here in this cycle of experience. Imagine that your higher self knows which decisions you *should* make in order to fulfill your own destiny while here in this lifetime. With this knowledge, and having your best interests at heart, it will try to, albeit subtly, influence your decisions according to your own best interests as determined by your path on which you walk.

Of course, you could have overruled your higher self and picked train number 1. Ultimately, you are in the here and now, so you can take your own lead according to your own free will. Who is to say that if you did take train number 1, then in several months, you wouldn't be faced with a similar scenario whereby the outcome could have been the same as that had you taken train number 2 in the scenario just mentioned?

I know that this concept may be hard to grasp or embrace, because it requires accepting the notion that you are connected to a source of intelligence external to your physical self that you may have no conscious knowledge of. And of course, this connection may not apply to everyone. Maybe your path requires you to try to detach from your higher self in order that you can experience events in a manner that could be construed by others as being mistakes.

All I would say is maybe just ponder this concept, and give it a while to truly sink in. If this notion starts to make sense and resonate with you, then great. If it does not, then worry not. Maybe, just maybe, part of your cycle of experience here includes not being able to be conscious of this higher version of your own self, for reasons that may become apparent to you in another time and place.

As ever, there is no hard-and-fast right or wrong answer, as our realities are according to our own perceptions, and our perceptions are according to what we are open to feeling and sensing. The best feeling to have or notion to accept is just being open to everything, whether you can see, touch, or smell it or whether you can just feel it. Being open to all potentialities does not mean you need to accept all potential outcomes, yet allowing theories that you may not have previously considered to enter your frame of thought may just start a cycle of events that leads to something happening to you that you would have never expected.

11

Connection to Source

What do I mean when I refer to "source"? Well, its meaning will depend largely upon what your own beliefs or perceptions are in relation to the ultimate intelligence that is responsible for all that we sense and feel. For me, "source" refers to the grand intelligence that is behind our presence here. Personally, I do not think of source as being a person or a physical entity in singular form. Rather, I perceive such as being an omnipresent form of infinite energy that has no static physical formation but that permeates through all living things. I do not think that in our current understanding, the source can or indeed should be defined. Rather, it can be felt. Thus, I try to refrain from assigning a name to such, because I do not think letters and words can adequately give sense and understanding to source, but rather the feelings that we have when we think of this source can be so much more profound.

I do not believe that in our current physical form, we are able to fully comprehend or visualize what source actually is. Although I do sense and feel that all life has indeed originated from this infinite and immeasurable energy, we are not able to remember the true form of such an energy and ultimate intelligence, because during this lifetime, it seems that we are to experience feelings and emotions that can only be experienced in, and are unique to, this particular destiny or reality. It is almost as if we can sense a very deep and very profound connection but we have been deliberately cut off from it in order to allow greater experience in this particular reality and perhaps also to find a route back to this connection while we are here.

I do believe passionately that the soul is indeed able to reconnect to source. But such a process of reconnection can perhaps only be achieved following a very genuine desire to look within for such a connection.

However, that is not to say, of course, that we do not sense this connection, often from a very early stage in the development of our physical bodies. Many people who sense this feeling align such thoughts and feelings to common overlays of currently accepted understanding. The untouchable and immeasurable link and connection to source is so profound that our souls actively seek answers, having forgotten them at birth, to what or who is behind this very powerful yet very subtle draw of what can be described as divine love and profound understanding.

It is almost as if we have been cast adrift in the ocean of physical experience, yet deep down we know that there is more to what is, other than just the vessel in which we currently find ourselves. We may not have what you might indeed call traditional proof, yet the fact that we are in this vessel is testament to the probability that there is indeed much, much more beyond that which forms the visual horizon.

But as often seems to be the way here, such principles of innate connection do not apply universally to all. Some people may not feel or sense this connection at all. But then who is to say that perhaps your own path, during this particular cycle of experience, is based upon having such experiences with no sense of feeling any connection whatsoever? Of course, accepting this hypothesis means also considering, at least, that perhaps the soul has some element of intended desires, ambitions, and goals before coming here to this particular island of reality.

It might be hard to really accept such a thought and notion into your mind without some sort of negative feeling being attached to such a possibility. For example, with so much negative energy being felt by so many people in so many different ways, it is beyond our range of comprehension and understanding to be able to accept or be open to the notion that we, in some manner, seek out experiences (not events) that find our timelines. Of course, I do feel strongly that this hypothesis may not be the case in all scenarios, and I would in no way suggest that such a theory is

100 percent accurate. There are, I am sure, events and experiences that we do not seek but that nonetheless still find our timelines.

Yet when I look back on some of the negative events and experiences that have happened during my own cycle of experience, I can see now what the feelings and emotions that I felt during those moments of positive and negative catalysts meant for the growth and development of my own understanding and relative perceptions. At the time, in the moments as they were presented via the catalytic experiences that occurred, all I felt was mainly anger, frustration, and sadness at what I was experiencing and toward what I was witnessing. But as I have grown in a spiritual sense, I can almost understand why the events occurred. Not because I have any control over the events but because the feelings that came before or after such events were the outcome of the aforementioned experiences, and it is those feelings that I can understand (now) as having some influence on my own perspectives and development as I have progressed through this particular timeline.

I am always quick to point out that of course I do not have any proof for such a hypothesis. But then there is no proof against it. So ultimately, it depends on what your own perceptions and feelings are on such matters. I also do think that experiences or events do indeed happen that cannot, at present, be afforded any kind of rational understanding, because such events are so painful either physically or emotionally that it is almost impossible in the here and now to make sense of them. So perhaps in such a scenario, such events or their reason(s) for occurring will make sense to us only at a place and during a time that are very different to those in which we currently find ourselves.

But what about connecting the previously mentioned source? Personally, I would advocate, while still being mindful of the teachings by fellow souls who surround us, to always go within when desiring to connect. I have studied, albeit not in much detail, many different religions, and in fact I embrace them all, and the very important messages that they carry and convey. I may not accept some sections of this civilization's teachings of such religions, but I DO embrace all religions as being important to the initial phases of the development of the soul. But that does not mean I have necessarily used such teachings as a means of connecting to my own affinity with source.

Rather, I have spent twenty-four years meditating (not constantly, of course), remaining open to all that occurs in this environment, and pondering what source means for my soul on a personal basis and how I am able to connect with such. And in doing so, I have become truly open to all suggestions and teachings, some of which resonate with my own understanding and some of which do not. But in essence, my own truths have been found internally rather than externally (i.e., by my own inner contemplation rather than what a fellow person has told me). Such a rationale has worked well for me. It may or may not work well for you.

Ultimately, I would say that for as long as you trust your own instinct on such matters, and you are 100 percent comfortable with such a picture that is drawn by your own instinct, then so be it. I look around the world now and see things that make me feel that those souls behind such things do what they do because they feel it is the right thing to do. Yet I cannot help but wonder whether really they do what they do because another human soul has hijacked their own eternal and very powerful links to source and manipulated such connections to further its own agenda.

Again, these are just my thoughts based on observations and feelings. Each of you will have your own such thoughts and feelings based largely upon your own observations. All I would say is that when another person tells you his or her own truths, then it would be prudent to remember that such truths are based upon his or her own perceptions and interpretations of the world around us. Yet we each have encoded within us the mechanism that is needed in order to be able to find our own connections to our own unique truths and understanding.

In summary, connecting to source is something that is unique and personal to each soul that roams this reality and that has come here for such a purpose. There are no right or wrong answers but rather methods and

JJJ

experiences that are unique to you but that may play a vital part in your own process of connecting to that which many of you have a very deep and very personal sense of connection to. One of the hard tasks comes with trying to decipher that which resonates with you from the infinite amount of information and experiences that exist within this particular reality.

12

Meditative States of Understanding

Below are two examples of what I feel can be relayed when connecting to that which can be aligned to while in meditative states. I would encourage you to keep an open mind when reading the two sections below. The words contained therein may resonate with you, but then, of course, they may not. They are really intended to give you a sense of the fluid dynamic of information that could come when adopting a meditative and relaxed state of mind while being open to any possible source of information.

One of the reasons why I desire to share them with you is that perhaps having read them, those who have not yet tried meditation may then be tempted to try it so that they can also attempt to connect to the majestic ether that awaits the conscious presence of the soul.

Perceptions

This intricate & finely woven divine web of reality, is reflective of the pure & majestic love behind the true marvel of presence. Sometimes it is easy, to get caught up in the fog of distraction, that, albeit temporarily, takes the attention of our soul off the divine energy that we all feel.

Indeed, sometimes this separation is well warranted. It allows our soul, through the interaction of the senses within our physical body, to continue to experience that which can only be experienced 'here', on this planet, Gaia, during this moment, according to the constraints of the timeline in which we currently find ourselves.

To move towards a sense of self enlightenment, is to try and keep this divine energy, within our souls, held at the forefront of our minds at all times. Not at the price of leaving behind the feelings and emotions which we have come 'here' for, but to allow such feelings and emotions to index themselves into our physical experience.

The senses of our human body, can convey to us only that which we are able to experience within this cycle of life. To step further into the unseen, the unheard and the unknown, one must voyage deeper into the energy that drives our conscience. Concurrently, we hold love in our hearts, and we share the energy of this love with one another.

During these moments of reflection, we think not of personality. We think not of material gain, of money or of acquisition. Rather, we quietly contemplate the true foundation of understanding, withholding the urge, as dictated by the ego if such is present, to impart on others that which we see and feel as our own truths.

We do not necessarily need proof to quantify these thought process, yet, if proof is what your soul desires, then look around the physical world using your physical senses. Be open to the eternal energy so deeply entwined in all that we do…

By further considering the possibility, that there are a limitless number of potential realities, we allow the horizon of our perspective and field of view to voyage deeper into the field of the unseen. Mere contemplation, can allow one's soul to start to experience, via deep thought, the notion that there is no limit to that which can be experienced. During these periods of discovery, it is important to try and keep your soul firmly grounded, in order that it does not start to become detached from this reality in which we currently find ourselves. How your soul keeps it grounding, will be dependent upon that which you enjoy and which brings you peace, in the physical sense. However, by engaging in activities which you find pleasurable, your physical self may indeed stay attuned to our physical world.

As time, according to how we measure it during this 'reality', ticks by, we can postulate the intricate strings of all that which our current senses can process. Such processes, will not always be similar in understanding to those souls around you. Yet, such differences are a key catalyst, if used correctly, to the onward journey of your soul via the exploration of experience, both via self, and other selves.

Of course, we should always be cautious of that which surrounds us, that attempts to sway the journey & path of our soul. For, this society, as a collective, may not yet quite ready to adopt the general mass-enlightened sense of understanding that helps our collective souls vibration to reach new phases in understanding. Not yet. In time; yes. But not necessarily on this period of understanding. Indeed, we can gather together, free of ego, in groups such as the Council of Enlightened. We can ask deep and meaningful questions about this particular reality in which we find ourselves in this moment of time. We can share information. Share insights and perspectives, yet, this process of exchanging information can only truly thrive with the notion of free will and wider acceptance. These are notions which take time, patience and work to fully embrace, according to their full potential. There appears to be no single 'golden answer' to a single question. There are, instead, many finely woven elements of infinite 'truth' which, taken in singular fashion, may shine only a small beam of light onto a vast, vast surface of varied realities.

However, as you start to piece and splice these narrow beams of shining light together, you shall start to sense that the area on which your beam of light shines, is part of something that is beyond the context of mere words to be able to explain. It exists. It is there. It waits for you to find it, and it shall embrace you when you do.

The divine 'keys', towards a greater sense of deeper understanding, lay closer to your soul than you may think. They lay there, waiting for you to pick them up, when you are ready. Find them, and they shall open up new spiritual doors & understanding. These doors of which I speak, may not be obvious to you at first. They are subtle in their composure & existence, yet entry through them allows for a profound sense of deeper exploration.

JJJ

As more and more souls become reconnected to that which we were once all connected, the vibrational effect of Gaia shall open new perspectives of awareness and experience. This task is not easy, because it was never meant to be. Controlling one's thoughts, one's fear and one's direction, is not only a requirement to further such voyages of discovery, it is also an effect of such. The two notions are hand-in-hand and form a close unity of defined experience.

It is essential, to quiet the mind, in order that the mind can connect to the essence of love and being, that permeates all that which has a life force within it. If, when you look at a plant, or an animal, or another human being, you feel this life force, then you are on the way to helping to open a new state of existence and understanding which allows all shared experiences to be had, whilst maintaining a sense of knowledge that the experiences which are indeed being had, form a close unity with the path that your soul foresaw before you came 'here'.

Our Souls gather together, because we remember. We remember that which has been forgotten and which has been buried under the layer of control which has, for so many years, been an effective instrument in the tool box of slumber. That time, has had its prime. Many souls which came before us, understood that which we are connecting to, and were put to physical pain because of such an understanding and connection. Many before us, have desired to share that which each of you feel, in order to awaken those from the slumber, yet, the technology was never there to enable such teachings to be passed in a fluid and undistorted fashion. Yet, this time is upon us, and this chapter is no mere coincidence.

In order to connect, to the many civilizations which exist and which also voyage towards the greater understanding but who are currently beyond the field of view of our physical vision, we must first develop our existence to a stage and level that will play host to those whom have also been through that which we are going through. As you take your younger loved ones by the hand, in order to guide them to love, so too are our hands guided by that which waits for your conscience to find it, as guided by love, and as illuminated through light.

Believe in your ability. Believe in your mind. Believe in yourself, and take this belief, hold it before you, and allow it to draw your soul to the path for which you came here for.

The Tide of Change

The eternal light from the new era, continues to gain in its divine luminescence. The momentum of change, continues to gather pace in a gradual yet measured manner. There are those of you here, in this time & place, who can indeed feel its presence. Your soul, shall perhaps start to remember more and more, in relation to that which came before, and that which comes after.

However, it is still vital to remain grounded and to keep your soul in fine balance. It is still vital to ensure that the essence of experience is still fulfilled, for the change is not meant to halt the experience, rather it is set to heighten it. The experiences which come with the new era of understanding, are set to bring about a harmonic melody that plays the divine tune, as generated by the orchestra of source.

Each second that passes in this illusion of time, brings in more energy from the source of that which stands behind all that ever was, is and will be. The boundary of your perception, may start to widen at a gradual pace. For, there are no shortcuts. To take such a shortcut, is to leave out a piece of the puzzle which is vital to the understanding of the bigger picture.

Keeping the focus of love in your conscious minds, is a vital part of knowing which piece of the puzzle fits into the correct layer, relative to your sense of innate understanding. If ever you feel unsure of that which I speak, then go quietly within. Ponder the essence of your understanding, so that perhaps new bridges are built within the dynamic of the physical mind.

Eventually dear friends, the network of information shall find the bridges which are built within your mind, until such time as they find their center in your physical worlds.

The transition of knowledge, is not an easy one to make. At times, the falsity of doubt may indeed act to question the understanding which you have. Yet, this environment is conducive to such feelings, because such allows the unique experience of physical catalyst within this realm to play its part.

Science is changing. That which was once held to be folly, shall start to form the basis unto which a new chapter of reality shall be formed. The opposing polarities of the esoteric, and the scientific start to narrow. The convergence of combined perception, shall mean that a whole new and exciting presence shall be felt by all.

Worry not, if those around you are yet to engage with this new wave of heightened awareness. Such a task of mass initiation shall find this sphere when the critical mass of awoken souls starts to vibrate in harmonized synchronicity to the wonders of all that is.

My dear friends; fellow souls to whom there is no separation, we are ultimately as one. We reflect the mirage of the illusion, according to our perception of that which we feel. As we start to feel a deeper connection, so too will the mirage of reality start to manifest according to that which we can project as a collective unity of love.

As each minute of time, as measured in this reality, passes by, take in all that which resonates with your divine and beautiful souls. Feel the warm glow of that which desires for our faces to be lit as we move out from the cold, into the warm.

13

Principles of Attraction

My own understanding, based on the experiences that I have had to date, regarding the mechanics and principles of the current reality in which we find ourselves is that when you strip away the physical layers, you are ultimately left with pure, and perhaps eternal, etheric energy. I am no scientist, and so I cannot with any affirmation give accurate scientific statements or observations in relation to that which I feel, sense, and understand. Yet I do sense strongly that although science can indeed describe the nature and form of the arena in which we currently find ourselves, it cannot currently accurately describe the principles of the events that occur inside of the metaphorical arena.

Science is so very important to our sense of understanding. It allows us to view the disposition of the various physical components of that which makes up our current physical reality. Without the frontiers of science, we would be merely floating on the oceans of experience, without understanding how the vessel that carries us actually functions. We would be adrift, floating on the winds of human interaction but not actually knowingly heading toward a specific destination.

But here, at this moment as I write this book, I am concerned with the form, function, source, and flow of the energy that inhabits the physical form. I guess some would call this energy to which I refer the life spirit or maybe spirit. I am intrigued and have spent the last twenty-four years of my life trying to comprehend the omnipresent layers of varying energy that not only give rise to our current physical form but also give rise to other manifestations of physical form, both that which resides on this particular planet and that which resides off this particular planet.

When you picture in your mind the energy associated with the soul, you can almost sense and feel the vibration of that energy. Almost as if there is indeed something that cannot be measured, detected, or manipulated via physical interaction but nevertheless still is so obvious that it would be folly to ignore it or to dismiss it.

Visualizing this sphere or ball of energy, we can almost sense its gentle and very subtle pull. Let us imagine that the energy of, for example, the soul is made up of positive, neutral, and negative states. Let's assume also that these various polarities can and do attract similar energies to the current composition and dynamic energy of the soul. For example, positive attracts positive, negative attracts negative, and neutral allows both positive and negative to be attracted to the sphere of energy that is the soul.

Taking the notion of the positive energy, let us assume that such a state of polarity is indeed held for more than just a few moments of time. It is my understanding that such a polarity will act as a beacon for events that have the same polarity; thus, positive energy and positive polarity can indeed attract events and experiences whose net outcome is also positive.

Of course, such a practice will not mean that only events leading to positive energies will occur. I sense this because I do not believe that the current arena in which we find ourselves is configured in such a manner so as to allow 100 percent positive experiences 100 percent of the time. It is my feeling that such realities can and do happen but that they are some way off in our journeys of spiritual development and understanding. Assuming also, of course, that some experiences are also predetermined, then such a theory would mean that even if you were able to maintain a 100 percent positive polarity, then negatively polarized events would still find your timeline at some point or another.

But then, depending on how well you are able to balance the polarity of your soul after catalytic events, then such will also depend upon what positives you can take from negative occurrences and what negatives you can also take from positive occurrences (the latter being a method by which you can also keep your energy or soul balanced during moments of extreme bliss—although you may not actually want to undertake such a balancing during such moments!).

Within the council's YouTube channel, there is a short video that gives some brief explanation in relation to my perceptions on the above principles. You may have to excuse the quality of the content, as video production is not my forte. As ever, it is never the aim or desire of the council, or therefore of myself, to give a definition in relation to any of the subjects that are covered.

I do not feel that it is the place or indeed the job of any fellow human within this particular reality in which we find ourselves to give authoritative dictations of such topics as those that are covered in this brief introduction to the esoteric, but instead we can each give guidance to one another, based upon our experiences and perceptions, which can indeed aid in the relative development and understanding of other souls.

We can teach what we know, but we should not attempt to make such teachings truths in the minds of others. Such practices only act to curtail the development, exploration, and experiences to be had by the billions of souls in the thousands of different life-forms that currently occupy this particular island of reality.

In essence, we can all learn from and teach one another. To listen is, of course, not necessarily to agree. Yet the more experiences that we listen to, and the more events that we ourselves experience directly, then for as long as the soul is balanced, it seems to me that our spiritual growth and understanding will indeed blossom, as it has been yearning to do for so many years, both collectively and individually.

And of course, this is one of the primary functions of the Council of Enlightened. Members desire to become enlightened as to their own realities, but in sharing information in an open and accepting manner, then such information, experiences, perspectives, and thoughts can precipitate through the conscience of the many to help enlighten the souls of all.

14

The Acceptance of All

Accepting, in principle, thoughts, experiences, rationales, ideas, and beliefs that may not resonate with your own current understanding can be quite a difficult concept and notion to embrace. And it is understandable as to why. If you believe something that, for example, you have been taught for decades by those whom you trust and love, then it is quite natural to become defensive when someone or something suggests something that goes against that deeply and genuinely held belief.

Often, people quite naturally become very protective and emotional over their own beliefs and their own unique understandings, owing in part to perhaps the fear that may be felt if entrenched beliefs are called into doubt or called into question. Of course, the protection of one's own beliefs has been the cause of many a conflict in the past and, of course, in the present. The urge we feel, often originating from deep within the ego, to defend our beliefs and understandings can be an extremely powerful and potent energy.

It is almost as if the emotions that are bestowed upon us in this particular reality become so infused with such beliefs that they (the emotions) feel a strong desire to defend such beliefs or convince others that our own beliefs should also be their beliefs. Yet when you purge the ego, you will find that the need for such a response dissipates completely. It is almost as if all the doors in the corridor of life suddenly open, and your soul then gets a glimpse into each of the doors in an attempt to further its own understanding.

For me personally, I never dismiss anything just because it may not resonate with me or my own experiences to date. With so many different souls in so many different forms having a limitless amount of experiences, it is virtually impossible to conceive that every one of those souls will form the same parallel understanding and the same perspectives from this infinite sea of infinite experience within infinite realities.

Therefore, I genuinely do accept and respect all views and perceptions that are shared with me. Nothing is too farfetched or inconceivable. Indeed, if someone does not agree with my own views or perceptions, then rather than try to defend them or substantiate them, I will take the view that another's path will display to that person a different scenery from, in this example, my own path. Just as when we walk through the same woods or forest, we see different things depending on where we are looking, so too do we build different beliefs based upon what we experience during this cycle of life. I have found that adopting such a view of openness and purging my ego negates any need for me to defend my own beliefs and understanding based on my own personal experiences.

As a very crude and basic example of this, imagine two fish living in the same ocean. One fish lives in the deep and very dark abyss and never sees the shining rays of the sun. The other fish dwells in depths where the sunlight still reaches it. The deep-sea fish will have a completely different perspective of the environment in which it lives and exists from that of the shallow-water fish, yet they live in what is essentially the same place—they just experience it in a different way. If they could talk to us, then they would describe their surroundings completely differently.

Yet as observers who are aware of both environments, we would therefore be able to resonate with each description of essentially the same place. There would be no need for the fish to defend their own perspectives based on their own experiences, as each one is based entirely upon how they interact with and where they reside within their own environments.

This rather crude and simplistic example is really just a way of illustrating that what we believe based on what we experience is really down to the manner in which we interact with and interpret the environment in which we find ourselves. Of course, essentially, the arena may be the same, yet the area immediately around us may be completely different—so-called islands of reality.

Let us also imagine that when one person tries to tell another about what his or her own beliefs are, the person precedes each such statement with the words "in my perspective" or "according to my own understanding." I am very confident that just with these select few and carefully chosen words, the statement that would follow such words would not have the effect of stirring the need for a defensive response in the individual listening to such a statement, assuming that, of course, such beliefs did not align with one another.

As simple as it sounds, I believe that this method of communication and interaction can actually have a profound effect and outcome on the manner in which we all interact on a day-to-day basis. For example, if I said, "Reincarnation is real; we live many lives in order to gain the experiences that we determine at a time and place that is utterly separated from the world in which we find ourselves," then those who do not believe in reincarnation might, whether in their own thoughts or verbally, feel the need to rebuff such thoughts, based upon their own experiences.

Yet if I said, "In my own understanding, based on my own experiences, that reincarnation is real; we live many lives in order to gain the experiences that we determine at a time and place that is utterly separated from the world in which we find ourselves," then chances are rather than feeling the need to defend a perception or viewpoint that differs from the above, the person who does not agree might simply say or think, "Well, that's not what I personally believe," rather than just saying, "You are wrong."

Maybe try this method of thinking next time you are having a conversation with someone who has beliefs completely opposite your own. You do not have to physically be in the same room as this person; it works just as well if you are watching something on TV or on the Internet. Even if the person you are listening to or viewing does not use the words "in my perspective" or "according to my own understanding," just imagine that he or she does. You may find that your desire to defend your own beliefs or understanding almost disappears immediately.

I do genuinely and honestly feel this means of interacting with people who have had a completely different journey from your own thus far can allow for an open forum in which ideas, thoughts, experiences, and perceptions are shared in a manner that does not create any significant or substantial negative energy and thus can have completely the opposite effect of such negative energy and may indeed actually help to broaden the perspectives and understanding of those privy to such discussions, rather than cause a scenario whereby one feels the need to defend one's own beliefs, ideas, and understanding.

Of course, accepting others' views is not the same as agreeing with others' views. But you would be amazed and surprised at what may grow when a seed of thought or an angle of perspective is presented to you that perhaps you may not have considered before. Indeed, such an acceptance and open-mindedness is vital to initiating and advancing along your own path to self-enlightenment. For we cannot truly explore the unknown unless we are willing and able to accept the possibility that all perceptions could also be, and become, all realities.

15

Question Time

So what of the questions and answers that follow? What is their purpose, and what do the answers mean for you and your own journey within this cycle of experience, if indeed they do mean anything to you at all?

The questions themselves are specifically formed in an attempt to try to aid those who are in the process of awakening to a new sense of understanding and acceptance. During this process of awakening, you may feel alone, or you may have people around you in whom you can confide as to the thoughts and feelings that you are having and are yet to have and experience. Some of the questions and answers given may resonate with you, and some of them may not.

Do not be worried or concerned if none of the questions and the responses that are given resonate with you, because it could indeed just be that the inferences within them are out of synchronicity with your current path in this particular time and place. You may end up reading all of the questions and answers and not draw anything of significance from them at all. Again, do not be perturbed if indeed this is the case.

However, you might conversely feel a deep connection and affinity with the words that are shared below. They may act as a beacon of understanding, showing in fact that you are not alone on this journey and that you are not alone as you wake up to the surroundings in which we currently find ourselves.

I have not edited any of the answers that have been given, because to do so would interfere with the intention behind the soul that uttered them. Free will must function, for as long as this free will does not create an imbalance within the finely tuned makeup of a neutrally polarized equilibrium, then it shall flourish and it shall unify to form new senses of collective understanding.

Below is a list of the eleven questions that were posed spanning over a time period between 2015 and 2016. This will enable you, if you so wish, to seek a question that was posed that maybe has a specific resonance for you at this moment in time. The initials of each member of the council are used so as to protect the identity of the contributor.

Confidentiality is key to the operation of the council, and hence it is something that I take quite seriously. Members shared their innermost thoughts on subjects that are quite different from the normal way of thinking.

Ponder also that each member is enlightened as to different notions, beliefs, acceptances, understandings, and states of awareness. Therefore, there are many, many different levels to enlightenment of the self and enlightenment of the whole. No member of the council claims to be 100 percent enlightened, and as has been mentioned above, I am not even sure that 100 percent enlightenment to ALL, as opposed to the self, is possible during this particular cycle of experience.

Q1: What initiated the events leading up to your awareness?

Q2: What has been your biggest hurdle thus far during your journey of awareness?

Q3: How has your life changed since your awakening?

Q4: During your journeys thus far, what has been the most profound unexplained event that you have experienced?

Q5: What has been the single most profound act of pure love that you have witnessed so far on your journeys?

Q6: Since becoming aware, what is your biggest concern about the future, and how do you balance this concern within yourself?

Q7: What do you feel is preventing more souls from awakening and learning about their own paths?

Q8: What would be your advice to give to a soul that perhaps feels lost and disconnected from its path?

Q9: How do you envisage the future of this planet in one hundred years' time, and why?

Q10: What advice to other souls would you give in order to help them find inner balance and inner calm?

Q11: If you could know the answer to any one single question, what would the question be, and why would you seek the answer to that specific question?

Q1: What initiated the events leading up to your awareness?

PW: In my case it's the training of coaching that I received that made me go fully into that process of awakening.

But as far as I remember, I was always keen on self development without knowing why I was so att.racted. I was intuitive without knowing it.

So where does it come from? I can't answer yet...

QQ: A wonderful idea smile emoticon The events in my life leading up to awareness were not of my choosing - in fact, I did much to avoid them! But as always happens, if you are of interest or needed in service, you receive multiple chances to take up your seat. For me, I finally relented when I had attended a spiritual meeting with the very purpose of stopping the experiences I was having. What I was taught instead was control over them, and from there, I was given encouragement to explore further. Once I had an element of control, my curiosity took over smile emoticon Q

KG: My event that initiated my awareness wasn't so lofty. Like many, I had to learn via suffering rather than wisdom. Through my divorce, and the heartbreak that followed, I was able to work through a lot of issues of ego fears, and therefore became aware of a greater part of myself, and that part's connection to all others. But this took a lot of sitting in negative emotions and not running from them. I made the decision after this to try to learn via wisdom - i.e. not make the same mistake twice! Yet before all this, I was aware of being different - of having a strong sense of authenticity and a natural belief in the spirit world, and a strong drive to face my personal issues head on.

KS: It's so synchronistic that this was asked rt now. I just finished writing a 6 part blog series on this and I'm about to start a wrap up post that will go into detail on my perspective of the whole process. I was going to post it here too to share. I think it may be too long for u to post in your book but I'll leave that up to u

AM: In my case, I was never really sure what I wanted to do in life. I was always teased and picked on when i was younger. So i really stopped talking to people unless I had to. I would just stay in the house. As I got older I had to do a few jobs that required a lot of physical labour. I knew that i didn't want to have to do physical labour or work for the rest of my life. To ensure that I would have a great job, I decided to enrol in college immediately after I graduated high school. I worked at bakery from 2 am - 8 or 9 am 5 days a week. when I got off I would then would go home, clean myself up and head to school. I had trouble retaining a lot of the information from class, as i was so tired from work. As an empath t was very difficult feeling a lot of the negative energy around campus. I began smoking marijuana occasionally to cope with my feeling of being alone and stressed. Soon, I found myself smoking weed several times a day. By the time my junior year came around my G.P.A wasn't that great.. At this point I was basically working just to smoke weed, I would fall asleep in class, skip class to smoke weed. I ended that semester with 4 Failing grades, and was put on academic suspension for a semester. I had reached an all time low. I felt like the dumbest person in the world and i began to drinking alcohol and smoking cigarettes. Christmas rolled around and my mom wanted me to come home and i wouldn't, I felt as if I didn't deserve it. I finally decided to move back in with my mom in January. She gave me this book that she had always been raving about, I never cared to hear about any of her spiritual books, let alone read one. Something inside of me wanted me to read the book, my mom told me to just read a page or two, to see if I like it. So I began reading "Conversations with God book 1" it was so great that I finished the entire book that night. While i was reading I felt a huge relief. Soon after i realized that I didn't need or want any of the toxins I was putting in my body. I then read book 2 and 3 the same week. I put certain habits behind me and never looked back.

LDJ: It all started in my youth. I already knew at an early age that I didn't fit in here. At school from day 1 is was bullied and this took place during my entire school time. It became less of course during the years but it had a long after effect of insecurity.

In my jobs I was very loved by my co-workers and my bosses were always very happy with me. In my personal life I went through a lot of experiences what brought me to this awareness. When I came on earth I had made the choice to experience all I had to do through relationships, lovers, friends, family, kids. I basically experienced the teachings of my book of life. I had a personal coach/spiritual teacher who helped me raise my awareness through opening my eyes how everything in this world worked. How everything that happened is a gift, and that it is all about my own reaction to events happening in my life. In this life I faced a lot of pain from other lives. Events that happened over and over again in many lives and I was never able to live with. But now I did. I had to become unattached to anything, anyone in this life, including "my" children. So the events leading up to my awareness started already in grade-school and continued during my life through all the relationships. All reflections of what I had to face in this life and sometimes still am facing, and life is one big adventure so more events will be there to experience.

JL: Great posts smile emoticon This will be among the few times I have recounted my initiation. I believe it started because of who I was, like Linda's childhood, I was bullied and felt out of place, out of my time. I was sensitive to my surroundings and the world turned me inwards, where I produced an anger against myself and strong fears of what was to become of me. This then went on into my teenage years as I formed dependent relationships with whomever drifted towards me, until in high school when in freshman year I was suspended for 10 weeks, an A+ honor student, for having less than a GRAM of marijuana on me, a substance which I was just buying for the first time in my life. Facing myself, this began the slow process of finding out who I was. Thanks to the International Baccalaureate program at my school, I finished out with a great education and "questioning attitude" that lead me into college with a thundering pace. My real awakening happened so fast, just this year I would say, as I finally accepted my own natural idea of love, which has now found itself in every root of my being through my own courageous acceptance of everything that is, has been, and will be. Thank you for letting me share

BM: I will express the reason i did not wish to publicly answer this question is simply i do not wish people to feel any amount of sorrow or any amount sadness for me, i will begin from the beginning and by the end of this you will understand exactly why i say everything in my life lead me to the point of my awakening.

At the age of 2 year 1989, i had woken up before my mother and her boyfriend at the time, i walked inti the living room and noticed a soda cup on the end table beside the couch, i also noticed a lighter next to the cup with my mothers cigarettes, i picked up the lighter and took the straw from the cup, i lit the straw on fire and watched in amazement as it melted in my hand, it then dripped onto my hand burning me, i then dropped the straw on our couch and it ignited the couch and before i knew it the entire house was engulfing in flames, i ran to wake my mother and she told me frantically to run outside, and i did.

My mother and her boyfriend jump out of the bedroom window because they got surrounded by flames, (this is what they told the firefighters). I watched as my mothers boyfriend ran inti the house multiple times thru the fire trying to save my younger sister who was only 6m old, the last time my mothers boyfriend came from the house his arms had been so burned from him reaching into her fiery crib the skin was literally falling off them,

My sister died in that fire that night, and for many years after that my mother would take me to her grave and have me tie toys to balloons and send them to heaven to say i was sorry for killing my sister.

Islands of Reality

When i was 3 i watched my grandmother and step father shoot heroine in the living room of one of their drug dealers house, between 3 and 5 i had seen them do heroine, cocaine, meth, crack, and then some.

At the age of 5 my step father had been molesting me and my only other sister at that time, when i threatened to tell on him he hung me by my throat with a cloths line in my bedroom closet, he shut the door and left me hanging i came thru with my mother holding me crying, now you would expect a mother to react to this a certain way, but my mothers reaction was to kick me out of her house so she could be with my step father still, from this point i was passed from family member to family member until i was 9 years old

At 9 years old i finally got to move in with my real father and learn that he wasn't the man i had perceived he was, my father was a very brutal and controlling man, from 9 to 13 i got beat so bad with a belt that I literally bleed on some occasions, as these beating continued i became numb to much more than physical pain so he began what he called the breaking process, using mental and emotional manipulation to the point i was afraid to even breathe if i wasn't told to, as he did this the beating gradually got worse and with much more solid items such as fists,2x4's, wrenches, ect.. Untill finally at 13 he booted me out if his house,

Now at 13 i was already for the past few years contemplating life and existence, i went to live with my grandmother for about 7 months before being told i had to go back to my fathers, and that my father was a born again christian now .. Well regardless of his beliefs when i got back to his house i realized once the door closed nothing was different, it was just mask

By the time i was 15 i had already tried to take myself out of this existence 2 times failing both times, at this time i felt the only way to get this to stop is to run away from home,

JJJ

So i took nothing with me except my bicycle, and rode it 2 cities away approximately 35 miles in the middle of the night so i could go unnoticed,

I was homeless until i was 17 with nothing but time to contemplate reality and existence, but was having a very hard time understanding due to a lack of education because my father also pulled me out of school at 9 years old and i was able to go, by the time i was 17 i was a drunk and on every pill you could imagine doing many negative things to fill the void and cover the pain, and then i met this girl and had relations with her in turn getting her pregnant,

Now im a 17 year old alcoholic pill junkie about to have a baby so im freaking out literally, me and this girl get into an argument in her 2nd trimester, i go to leave in a van that was given to me, and she jumps in front of the van as im speeding off, due to the alcohol and pills that were in my system at that time i was unable to react quickly enough and i hit her with the van, in turn causing her to miscarriage, and killing what would have been my firstborn,

After this i locked myself in a house that a friend of mine owned, and stayed there for 2 1/2 weeks alone going thru withdraws because of the incident that played out with my firstborn,

It was in that 2 weeks i began to realize how much is really just in our physical minds

From 17 to 21 was a time of immense studies trying to understand everything, in this time period i also attempted to leave this reality but ever time i tried it didnt seem to work like i was cursed to live this dreadful life (no-longer my perception) with no way out, but it was also in this time frame i began to realize this ability that i was able to see everything about someone just by looking at them and also this amazing ability to see thru peoples lies, this intrigued me with a wonder of why and how,

At the age of 21 i had began meditating and had discovered what at the time i knew to be my spirit guide, and i was asking him questions and fallowing his answers which lead me to a website where i would an amazing person that gave me the link to the book of storms empath 101 i read this book and it explained everything that I questioned about how i was seeing these peoples pasts and thru their lies so easily,

It was this moment my awakening began and it has been 7 years to date since my awakening began and the i have since learned many amazing things about this existence,
   The most amazing being we can all at anytime be at peace if we just understand that we are truly in control

CA: In my case there were no initiating events per say that led to awareness/awakening. I was always aware/awake, for me my journey has always been about the exploration of who I am, I had the material available. It was about remembering who I am and to date one thing has led to another. I really think my mother knew, she did tell me I was going to have the hardest life of all. With all I knew I never fit in, I couldn't relate to others we did not speak the same language and they couldn't relate to me. I don't think I really understood this until grade 5. Someone had bought a Ouji board to school and I asked how you use it. According to their instructions you put your hands 5 inches above the device and it will move to give you an answer, well I followed the instructions they gave me it moved and gave me an answer to my question, I had to be pulled out of school for the rest of the year. Thinking about this is hilarious now and as a child well devastating. If I take my life and look at it from another perspective it definitely does not make sense and that's okay.

AR: I think its the karma from the past life why people are oriented towards the esoteric. I have always had this awareness inside me since childhood. When people around me would work hard towards achieving materialistic coals like marks in school as students or house or car as adults, I would think of meditations and mantra to know myself and the reason of my existence. I believe in a belief which is difficult to explain to people who are logical. There was absolutely no initiating event-painful or joyful. I guess the awareness was just carried forward to this life from the past life.

KR: I have always been slightly different but the moment of realization for me was one night when I was in the bath! I began thinking REALLY hard about death and what it was, what it meant and my fear about it. Then it seemed like I went macro and saw everything... like everything dawned on me and the shutters had been removed from my eyes! I felt really strange and panicked, and like my whole life had been a lie and the whole world was lying!! I felt like everything was SO much bigger than this tiny world. I started getting really hot and cold and felt sick to my stomach and felt like I was going mad!! Luckily I have a spiritual friend who was "awakened" (even though I didn't know what that was before!) and he told me that yes the things I felt were true and that a lot of people wait for this moment for many lives.... I was terrified!! I kept telling him that I must be going mad and what I was seeing/feeling couldn't be real! Since then more and more things are being integrated but that was the night everything changed for me!! That was about 6 months ago now and it's mad to think how before I was completely "in the dark"! It's taken me a while to adjust to my new "reality" but nothing about it feels wrong or untrue and so they are the guides I stick with! smile emoticon

MA: Hi - my own awakening came about following some work that I was doing for an overseas Government. The work that I was involved in meant that I had some interesting information that was used for scientific reasons. Some of this information, did not really have 'explanation' as we understand the meaning of such. So I started to think more about the nature of our reality; who we are, why we are here and what are we here for? I have not yet found these answers, indeed, I may not find them at all... But I seek further evidence of that which has no 'evidence' almost daily. For anyone who truly thinks that this life, is our only life, then I would ask them to provide evidence for such. And when that person asks me to prove that there are other worlds, other lives, other consciences, then I would say to them: next time you look into space. then there is your proof my friend - with a smile of course wink emoticon

YD: I saw energy instead of human interactions all around me..relationships..colleagues..friends..what I saw ...then I tried to put in words which was not enough....it is never going to be enough..because I was viewing it from the wrong perspective...

Q2: What has been your biggest hurdle thus far, during your journey of 'awareness'?

ES: Trying to be the witness, so i keep thinking about becoming the witness and the mind chatter never stops, and getting bored and frustrated. Second would be losing complete awareness of the present moment and entering day dreams

AS: Hmm.. Interesting question.. James you can attach my name to anything i say anytime you like:)

As far as what is the biggest hurdle? I would say along this path the hurdle has been and continues to be Urinating out the Illusionary Programmed Beliefs I once believed while ingesting a new Re-Programming of what I now actually believe to be true for me. This has been the human experience for me. Its going to the movie and believing what I'm watching is illusion and walking back out of the movie believing I'm walking back into reality. When now its the other way around so to speak if ya catch my drift:)

Now for me its hmmm what do I do now with this little information I have realized consciously? Where best to apply it that places me in a favorable position that brings me the highest level of excitement right?

Hmmm.. Decisions decisions decisions!! I guess ill let myself know when the moment is right.. Great question by the way..Thank you again:) Much smiling to you all:))

LW: So many wonderful creative minds coming together collaborating a body of work. I also look forward to our retreat and meeting our group! Supporting your vision! Great question! When you come into the earth plane with your lights on, the challenge comes to always remembering who you are and the purpose for you being here. Be of the world, not worldly. We are observers, way showers, peace ambassadors, light workers, spiritual teachers, and healers. Our unique soul signatures each form an important piece in the ascension plan of Mother Earth. Our journey here is to return to love, and to be living love in action. We are pillars of light and we are expanding our love and increasing our frequency for the greater good of all mankind. As students of life we embark on self mastery, soul mastery, life mastery, and love mastery in many shapes and forms. Transcending duality into oneness

JH: BEing present

KLT: The biggest hurdle for me..
    The ego

LDJ: My biggest hurdle is to be able to be and stay who I am. To stand for what I feel, to not let the opinions of others get in my way (ego). To not be afraid to express and be myself the way I am, no matter how others think about it.

CT: Going through a barrage of gurus who initiated me with secret mantras, wanting money, obedience, only to find out they had no realisation..

AB: Aside from general issues of mistrust for various reasons as possible obstacles, your question got me thinking about what really holds me back now. I go back to my own reference point. I've tried to previously describe my own 'quantum moment' of experience of 'higher awareness' that I once had. I have tried to descibe it from the separate thoughts that arose at the time. Those thoughts are what I remember and can describe as separate and distinct from the experience itself which was indescribable relating to awareness only. Like trying to describe a colour without pointing to something else that has that colour. For me it was a glimpse of a new dimension of possible exploration and 'being' I was completely unaware of before. I remember also thinking during the experience that what my senses were telling me was like what was 'out there' was somehow a reflection of me, but yet a feeling that something else lay tantalisingly beyond my conscious grasp. Like a forgotten word on the tip of my tongue. One thing I realised I haven't mentioned to anyone before, and I now realise that I had put aside from even my own consideration, is that I also remember in that moment that a feeling arose of being profoundly lonely, almost like a dread of realising that I was possibly all there is/was. Your question brought this forward to my mind and I pondered why I hadn't acknowledged this before and had almost forgotten about it. Have I been dishonest with myself? Have I since been distracting myself looking for any other possible way than facing this? I consider that perhaps at a fundamental level what maybe holds me back is facing this possibility. Perhaps this is a natural obstacle we all face at some level that we can overcome. Maybe it was a trick of the ego protecting itself. Perhaps I need to be more honest.

AM: My biggest hurdle has been discerning when others are open to receiving the deeper truths I want so much to share. On one hand, speaking my truth is living authentically and maintaining balance between my soul and my personality... but on the other hand, if I am speaking my truth to someone who will respond with resistance, then am I really helping? Should I not be more tactful and save my energy for truer connections, expressing gratitude for the souls I /am/ able to reach rather than mourning the ones I cannot yet commune with? But then if I do so, am I holding back? And is it out of wisdom and love, or out of fear and self-consciousness? And if it is the former, am I validated in my withdrawal because my intention is pure or am I to push those limits of a comfort zone? Which path of action will contribute a greater positive energy shift to our collective society?

As you can see there is still quite a bit of internal dialogue going on where integrating my awareness into my previously established connections with people is concerned.

I trust the answers will come the more I learn to let my intuition and inner light guide me and shed the layers of fear and ego -- ESPECIALLY ego -- that no longer serve me (or anyone else).

PS: My biggest hurdle has been relating to the others in my life who are sleeping. With that being said, I am thankful for you guys.

KS: For me it was learning to put myself FIRST. I had to stop thinking about the overall good of everyone around me, even those I loved, and just PUT ME FIRST. Once I finally understood putting myself first and loving me WAS loving everyone else, I finally understood it was never egocentric at all to do this and now I do it everyday. I've learned to feel and express gratitude for myself and feel the abundance of Love and Light in my life now that I've finally overcome this amazing hurdle! IT'S SO UTTERLY FREEING TO LOVE ME (ALL OF ME)! To have found and reconnected with my TRUE SELF once more is the connection I've been seeking my whole life!!

JBR: I have found my biggest challenges have been re-programming negative thought patterns (it takes work, dedication & time), learning to shield or not absorbing other people's negative energy & not letting my mood become altered by it. The hardest concept that I am still tackling is fully accepting that duality (the concept of good & bad) does not really exist.

There are some instances where this makes sense to me; that an experience is just an experience & it is the interpretation & perception of the mind's frequency that makes it positive or negative. But when applied to people or conscious beings for me, this is a tricky concept. We all have light & dark within us, it is natural law. From personal experience, I have encountered people & beings that are malicious in intent & not of the Light. I believe that there are people or entities that can be of the light or dark & I have not encountered many instances where a being is all one or the other. The trick for me is seeing that little spark of light, no matter how small, in others, to be able see yourself in them in order to have compassion, understanding & love for them regardless of their actions or intentions. I also personally believe no one is beyond redemption. It is of the power of free will & what a conscious being chooses in their actions that determines what type of being they are & whether the Light or Dark will dominate.

CA: For me it has been the realization that I have been lied to in all facets of my life that the history books have been changed to suit an agenda and coming to grips with that well it just wants to make me puke

QQ: My biggest challenge has been putting in the work required in my personality, so that I could connect with my soul. I was forced to drill deep into my personality, uncovering all of those demons that you hope no-one will notice. I struggled daily with being faced with who I am in this lifetime, but it was only by accepting these and acknowledging that these facets were absolutely connected with my personality and not my soul, could I then free myself enough to connect on a higher level. It is so easy to try to avoid working on your life here, particularly when you have been given a sign that there is more, but you are of no use if you miss that step. I stayed in my personality for a very long time and I nearly gave up. But at that moment of surrender, I would be reminded of my importance, and reminded that you are never given more than you can handle and that I COULD do this.

TS: My biggest challenge on this journey of self-realization... two nervous breakdowns which eventually became breakthroughs. I did not think I was going to make it at times. Very dark, very deep.

ANON: RESISTANCE !

AS: An airplane cannot take flight without first the resistance of the wind! smile emoticon Experiences are designed to show us what we WANT ONLY in life thus it being necessary. This is the Great Balance... The Power of Choice!

AW: The biggest hurdle thusfar in my journey towards "awareness" are the occasional failures in consistency in my practice, mainly in not following through meditation.

Question 3: How has your life changed, since your 'awakening'?

LDJ: Tremendously. Basically everything. Detached from everything and everyone.

AM: My life has changed beautifully since my awakening, every aspect of my life has improved. My understanding of the universe and everything in it is much clearer.

KS: My life has completely 180'd for the better! Everything is easier and happier! Life is a never ending carousel ride of love and forgiveness! I love life!!! ~No worries. Take care. BE Love!!!!

SM: Everything. From the perspective, to the emotions, modus vivendi, as Linda says... the strongest is the detachment, this is something not many relate even some that have awaken, but it is my feeling. I don't mind death because is not real, I don't fear it, I don't mind or care deeply if my family dies either, I'm not saying I don't give a damn but... I truly believe this is not like 'real', is temporary, it was my decision to be here I know, but it is about the learning experience, and I have that feeling towards several things. This is only a body, yeah I take care of it, but the spirit and the mind, my genuine essence is just craving to leave this place, to go back to where I'm/We are from. I just can accept the here and the now. Is just hard to go on with the everyday system illusion.

KG: It is so much more of an internal life now - which ironically allows for much more giving of my gifts to the outside world.

LD: The biggest change for me, I would have to say, is that I'm able to look upon a situation now, with compassion for ALL parties involved. For instance, if there was a horrible event that caused people to loose there lives at the hands of another human, I'm not in a position to ask " why" anymore. I simply accept that this was agreed upon by those involved, and for whatever those reasons are, I'm able to have compassion for even the most heinous criminal.

PL: the most noticeable change is the move from individualised self sustaining thinking to a non localised, multi levelled approach to every new situation as it arises. instead of trying to defend and get the most out of every encounter for yourself, you are able to witness the different views and perspectives that possibly exist at all moments. life no longer is about right or wrong, but instead understanding of just being. your self no longer strives for the pointless material and egoistic based rewards it has always driven for. the separation between mind and heart is now understood and the self no longer blindly follows what ever means to an end it seeks. Time becomes non existent, simple everyday moments shine with incredible beauty, and you view the world through lense of compassion and content-ness. you see the light shine through even the most troubled persons, you now exist only to ease the suffering of those around you and you strive to educate and further yourself in the things that really matter in true existence.

LIP: I am not afraid anymore.

I dare to stop with my job where I don't feel well, ready to go toward unknown ... I dare to love more und trust ...

I am ready and dare to love others and a man particularly.

I follow love and only love with Gods help.

QQ: I am less fearful. I spent a long time scared about what I was being shown, but once I was able to control it more, the opportunity to study myself and my soul to a much deeper level became an irresistible urge. I am able to understand this world and my place in it more easily, particularly when addressing situations that previously would have made me feel out of control - I now look at them as opportunities to learn and to burn the karma so that I may continue to move forward.

The most beautiful thing is in seeing the true wonders of the universe. I was so blinded by my own wants and desires previously, whereas now they run alongside my ability to just 'be' in the moment, and appreciate all that has been provided to me on my journey. Q

SM: Reading all of you makes me feel such a peaceful joy... Because everything you say either I've felt it or I totally agree. The acceptance and understanding lead us to unification and respect. Im glad I found you beautiful spirits. Thank you for letting me know that we are getting closer/together being so different yet United.

AB: To be honest, I tend to find the word 'awakening' as a bit ambiguous, meaning different things to different people. To me it seems to imply a state of before and after some kind of event or process. I feel there is always further to awaken to. Like an ascending ladder of rungs, perhaps leading ultimately to a state of unconditional love. I find people seem to have varying ability to communicate and hear each other depending on the relative number of rungs between them on this ladder of 'progress'. I myself feel my life has changed quite a bit from my earlier, more self centred days. A mostly gradual process with some prominent 'events' that have given me a boost/kick! I feel I have further to climb but I'm generally now able to take a more relaxed objective view of things. I seem to be able to take on advice and wisdom I previously seemed unable to hear or be able to internalise. I no longer get so ruffled at the mainstream nonsense going on. Choosing to focus more on supporting positive alternatives and strategies. I listen more and try to connect to others more effectively. I'm much more openminded and looking more for that which connects us rather than divides us. I've gotten better at recognising my own limiting beliefs and I'm more willing to let go of them. I'm becoming more able to come to terms with the ocean of unknown.

MHS: As I read the question I felt a bit shy to comment seeing I don't quite feel like I've actually awaken yet. To me, it feels more like it's a process, a long one. Through this path of awakening, the strongest feeling I get is of gratitude. I feel grateful for having been "shaken", for being made to look at the darkest spots of my soul with compassion and ease. I'm grateful for being on a the path that, having shown me my shadows, helps me be aware of any kind of judgment I might carry towards any being. I'm grateful for learning how to breathe and accept things as they are knowing everything happens the way they are supposed to. I'm grateful for the quieteness that helps me listen and foresee any negative reaction before I cause any harm towards self or others. I'm grateful for the paths that have lead me to communities such as this where I can learn and share so much with such wonderful souls as yourselves. I'm grateful and I hope to find a way to give a lot of love back to the our planet and the universe.

AM: I don't feel there is a final destination to being "fully" awakened. We are all constant learners and though we can (and should!) always seek to further understand, the perpetual mystery of what still remains unknown is part of what makes the awareness of individuals such as ourselves in this Council so precious.

To answer the original question:

There's not really a lot I could say that others haven't covered very eloquently and accurately, but here are my own words nonetheless: Since this process of awakening began, I have definitely gained a greater sense of interconnectedness and a much stronger ability to detach from my thoughts and emotions enough to see them with a wider lens. I've found strength and power in exercising unconditional compassion for myself and others. I've been able to slow my pace to savor & observe each moment. I've been able to tune into my intuition and trust that there is an answer to all things - and that even being unsure is an answer.

TS: My life had changed in ***EVERY*** way. Profoundly. More beautiful. More blissful

YBK: i look around end get spontaneous joy from little things like birds tweeting beautiful green plants en the full moonz energy...

AW: I am more aware of who I am as a being, and am continually building a more positive lifestyle around what I am learning about myself, helping myself and others in the process.

JL: From fear to love in all aspects. From personal to collective thinking. From living in worry to living right now. From fighting to accepting. This and much more grin emoticon love you all

ANON: The biggest epiphany I've ever experienced is the knowledge that everything in my life is my creation. WoW!!!!

Q4: During your journeys thus far, what has been the most profound unexplained event that you have experienced?

SM: Unexplained at first. The "messages". Those are, for me, intense, direct... always showing me 'the way"

SD: The powerful ways the universe speaks to you. Through synchronicity, beauty, the beings one meets on their path and dreams. To join in conversation with the universe is a beautiful and confusing thing. Confusing only because it speaks on it's own terms, and only when you let yourself flow with its waves, begin to manifest yourself on it's terms are you able to begin to understand. Even then, the multi-faceted nature of it ALL is a lot to comprehend! I'm always in a state of blissful bewilderment when I feel/listen/see/experience the universe's language, and see how powerfully she speaks through the experience of life.

PW: I was feeling very down, worried about my daughter's health, and her living situation. I became very emotional, I was crying and I called out to Goddess Isis to help my daughter, and to help me...I was questioning my path, wondering if I was where I am supposed to be. I asked to see where I had come from and where I was going. I took a sea salt bath, and closed my eyes to try to relax. I saw the Infiniti sign in bright beautiful shades of purple, lavender, and lilac. The sign disappeared and I saw wave after wave of beautiful purple colors, in the center of the waves of purple was a tiny twinkling light, like a star, it was bright white and appeared to shimmer in shades of gold and silver. A sense of peace came over me, like I have never experienced. It was so beautiful, I felt like I wanted to be there forever in that twinkling light and waves of purple all around me. My daughter recovered quickly after that, and although I haven't experienced that vision again, I will always remember it, and the feeling of pure peace.

PJM: I saw a beautiful Angel in my home. It was very large, light pink n baby blue, my favorite colors. I have vaulted ceilings so it was big. So beautiful and benevolent, and protection was the reason it came. Someone was being mean at the time, and her energy was so abrasive, I wouldn't answer when she called. My boyfriend took the call, it was his Mother. The Angel stayed for the duration of the call and left. Such pure graceheart emoticon I know in my heart it was a celestial being, but It didn't look like

Angels in paintings. It was more amorphous. The most amazing thing I've ever seen, and just that once. !

MHS: Back in January, right after I had started my journey and while devouring books on enlightment and love, I had a very lucid dream. I was floating, I felt indescribably peaceful. I remember feeling infinite love and utter bliss, I knew it was the expression of pure divinity, and inside my mind a voice kept telling myself "that's what our true nature is, that's what God feels like". I remember waking up with the awareness that "that's where we're supposed to return to".

LDJ: The experience of seeing parallel lives at the same moment. It confused me for a while, until I figured out what was going on.

KS: So far I haven't had any "unexplainable" events happen to me. The "knowing" of what is happening seems to come with each experience, although, I have had many profound ones. One of which was when I finally understood what it meant to fully love someone without any expectations or need for reciprocation. When that comprehension finally took root within my soul and I chose to love someone for the sheer desire to give and express Love because I wanted to, I felt Love returned to me from the Universe almost 3-fold. I felt the embrace of angelic and warm wings hold me while I quietly and joyfully cried and comforted myself. I don't remember how long it lasted but I remember falling asleep in this embrace feeling whole and completely loved for the first time in my life.

QQ: There have been many smile emoticon. My favourite is one I experienced a few months ago. I was meditating, and unusually I was laying down, rather than sitting. As I lay there, I suddenly saw the most beautiful white wolf, with piercing blue eyes, approach me and walk up my body, putting its nuzzle to my nose so I could feel the heat of its breath and I could see each strand of fur. It was awe inspiring. I knew I was in the presence of a higher energy, there was such a calmness and strength and wisdom. My beautiful wolf stayed with me for months, and even now when I need to make decisions, I feel him join me once more, curling around my legs in a silent display of support and commitment. He will not leave me and that gives me strength to trust my intuition. Q

FA: For me it was when channleing began.. i was both directly talk too threw another human unaware himself untill it was over. I have also been used to channle information too others. Mother earth, MU's, Annuaki, and universal awareness are a few too name..

CC: It's funny, but I experienced something like this just today. I have always felt a deep bond with Nature. Just gazing at the sky or feeling the breeze on my face used to give a feeling a bliss. But today I was taking a walk at the lake in the evening when all of a sudden I was just hit by the majestic beauty of the lake. I stood transfixed, staring at the lake, completely overcome by it's serenity. Waves of calmness and tranquility washed over me and I felt like I had become one with the lake. At that moment, I felt like the lake was communicating with me, telling me something that words cannot describe. And I felt that my soul was in harmony with Nature, with all of Creation. I felt like I was in on the secret. The secret of Creation. A secret code that governed the whole universe ie that we are all one, one with Nature, and one with all of Creation.

DS: I sawed in my dream while my sis was sis i was finding a cure for her i sawed a strange light and herad a voice say if you relly want her to be cure than she shall - when i woke up she was not sick she was sick in real life dying after that dream she was better

JJ: Thank you all, for sharing. I would like to share with you, one of my own experiences. A few years ago, my Grandfather passed away, in his sleep. His passing was peaceful. A few days after he left this 'time' and 'place', during a moment of quiet reflection, I asked myself "I wonder what time he passed away?"... I thought no more of it, and continued about my daily business. Several nights later, whilst dreaming, I woke up suddenly. I was on my own. I heard a very soft, and gentle voice, of what sounded like a female. The words uttered to my conscience were: "this is what time, your grandfather passed away". I looked at my watch, and it was 0330. A few days later, I spoke with my Grandmother, but did not mention this occurance of which I share with you all. I asked her what time the paramedics had arrived at their house. She mentioned that it was about 0730. After the funeral, I asked my mother if she knew how long prior to the paramedics arriving, had my grandfather passed on. She said that she had been informed by the Coroner that he had been dead approximately 4 hours. I share this experience with you, in dedication to my Grandfather, who is no doubt experiencing a different 'time' and 'place' to that in which we currently find ourselves.

JL: Wonderful comments! smile emoticon I cannot say that I have experienced a "most" profound experience, but many that all seem as profound and insightful as the last. Multiple times recently I have been involved in deep contemplation when at the same exact moment something happens around me (song lyric, conversation, event, etc) that is so synchronized with my thoughts that I have been filled with pure joy to the point of tears. All I have is gratitude heart emoticon

AM: This has happened to me exactly. So many seemingly "insignificant" synchronicities. The universe speaking to me in ways benign and inexplicable. So many separate events lining up in perfect cosmic communication.

AB: side from profound states of mind I quite often encounter odd events/synchronicities/dramas that seem to come out of nowhere. Their unlikeliness or oddness often strikes me as profound. My very first post on here back on 10th July 2015 was of my 'pigeon incident' which seemed particularly profound and unexplained. Another example of one that particularly sticks out, I remember when I was 12 once being in a beer garden with my parents and other friends, where us kids all played amongst ourselves whilst all our parents socialised. My mum had bought some raffle tickets and when it came time to draw the raffle she called me over, handed me the tickets and told be to go inside to the draw and see if we had won anything. There were 6 tickets. I was a bit miffed because I wanted to carry on playing with my friends, but also being quite shy at the time I didn't want to potentially have to walk up in front of everyone to collect a prize. I went inside and they began announcing the 6 main prizes for the draw to a fairly large gathering. I remember willing not to win to avoid the unwanted attention. They drew the first ticket. Of course, it was mine. I reluctantly went up in front of the cheers to collect my prize. Second ticket - mine again. A bit embarrassed, again I made the walk up to collect my prize. Third ticket - mine again, this time people calling "fix", my face red with embarrassment I collected my prize. Fourth ticket - mine again - lots of howls of "fix" while I collected my prize. Fifth ticket - mine again, by this time I was feeling highly stressed. The woman who was drawing the tickets asked me out loud if I should hand the prize back to give somebody else a turn. I just wanted to melt. I had to admit in front of everyone they weren't my tickets and I had to check with my mum. I went out to check with her, and she, oblivious to what had been going on, busy in the middle of talking, said "of course" I should claim the prize. I went back in, and accepted the prize to boo's and loud groans. The woman then asked I pick the final ticket for the last remaining prize, to ensure that it wasn't me that won and give someone else a chance. I put my hand in the hat, rummaged around the many tickets in there and pulled the final ticket - as she read it out, to my horror I realised again it was mine!! the crowd erupted. Nobody could believe it. At that point I asked if I could draw again, to a cheer, and somebody else won, and I made my escape with my 5 prizes. In this case, to me I felt as though I was being taught a painful lesson by the universe to not will for situations that go against me because of shyness. These kinds of 'unlikely' incidents have recurred throughout my life, often with a little lesson attached, sometimes not realised till later. They always seem very profound in a very personal kind of way.

ZW My answer to your 4th question is this; I was disheartened that my journey is filled with distractions and judgement, that I dreaded having conversations with my peers. A day after that, I received an invitation from you to join this council. It's such a sweet synchronicity

Question 5: What has been the single most profound act of pure love, that you have witnessed so far on your journeys?

LDJ: That experience just happened to me. I experienced several acts of love, but this one is so pure.... I am still out of words.... I want to go back to the Netherlands, to be with my kids again, to feel them, to hug them, to be with them for a while. The moment I was giving up on hope someone offered me to pay half of my ticket.... No strings attached...just an act of pure love.. I am so grateful..

QQ: I think it has been quite challenging to experience pure love in the physical realm, as there are so many competing energies and unless you are surrounded by others who are awake, that energy can deplete your ability to sense the love that emanates from within and around you. One of the most profound moments for me was at the gravestone of my grandfather - a man I never met, as he died when my mother was six years old. The family were somewhat estranged and so it took me nearly 40 years to go to the grave but eventually my journey took me there. As i looked at the stone, an overwhelming sensation of being hugged was all around me, and the love that I felt in that moment was breath taking. I could have understood it had i been able to love the man in the physical world, but to feel that surge of potent love from someone who I had never met was awe inspiring and I felt certain at that moment that we meet the souls of others many times and some may never meet in physical - but the connection is still there. Love of a hundred different personalities, wrapped into that one moment with the soul attributed to my grandfather was beautiful.

AP: It was happened twenty years back, one of my school mate was isolated in inner Dubai and he send an emotional letter after a break of fifteen years.

AB: Its hard to pick a single instance. Love appears in many forms to me. I feel it in the unconditional love between souls, in witnessing acts of selflessness, in the passionate commitment and dedication to pursuits such as fighting for justice, in art, in sport, in bringing an idea to reality, in mastery and creativity expressed through a skill. I'm not particularly religious but I remember once visting the Cook Islands whilst backpacking, and completely by chance somebody in passing had recommended we should go to the local church to hear them singing on Sunday. So a few of us backpackers went along (more for something to see and do, with not very high expectations if I'm honest). However, whilst singing along with the locals there I felt completely moved to tears by the overwhelming feeling the love in the place, the unexpected harmonies of their beautiful voices (a different class of singing from normal), the closeness of their community spirit, the perfectness of the weather and location, the very modest simplicity of the church, and even afterwards where the congregation had unexpectedly prepared a huge spread of food for us visitors, with a beautiful assortment of home baked food they had obviously spent some time, effort and care in preparing. They took a great care to make us feel so welcome without any expectation of anything in return. It was just a profound and very humbling moment for me, made all the more profound because of my own lack of expectation.

Question 6: Since become 'aware', what is your biggest concern about the future, and how do you balance this concern within yourself?

ANON: Thankfully, I have found inner peace since becoming more "aware". I used to be anxious all the time. I trust the universe and the Source; that everything will go as Its Plan.

PW: My worry is that since there seems to be a much greater number of 'aware" people embracing their feelings and beliefs in the last few years, I'm concerned that at the same time those that are not aware, are becoming increasingly aggressive and exhibiting more violent and brutal behaviours.

I try to concentrate on my path, go through the ups and downs that come with it, but try to stay focused on what I believe. Amid all that's going on, my concern is, how will this all end?

AB: I actually feel quite optimistic about the future. I feel my biggest concern has been my general perception of the awful injustice impressed upon the vast majority of life, and the danger to the environment that supports us, perpetrated by some kind of 'powerful hidden controlling force or ideology' hiding behind a false mask, amplified by the seemingly shallow lazy ignorance of the masses. I balance this perception with an understanding that there is very much that I don't and can't possibly know about, and therefore can't blindly take information I come across at face value to form any strong opinions. There's probably more disinformation out there than truth, but when the truth is encountered it will always stand firm upon further scrutiny. There is also a logic that such a fear based system/perception built on lies is completely unsustainable in the face of the truth. The increasingly vast multitude of new channels by which we all now communicate should make it increasingly impossible for any nefarious few who might benefit from such a system to keep tight control over and cause such biased mass perceptions in order to keep their secrets hidden. These new channels make it easier to receive a much broader stream of information from all points of view, and to be able to become increasingly exposed to and propagate new progressive ideas far and wide, enhance cooperation and collaboration, and to be able to recognise more of what we all have in common instead of our imagined differences. Only truth, love and cooperation are sustainable.

PT: I have no fears as i believe that everything in the universe is exactly as it should be. Without darkness there can be no light, and without pain and suffering, there would be no growth or experience to transform the human from animal to homoluminous...

ONJ: My belief is that the greatest concern is that there are more aware than unaware and that the souls that don't want to be aware will become violent:-

LDJ: No fear or concerns for me. All is as it is

CMB: My only concern is remembering who I am...other than that my heart tells me all will be as it should.

QQ: I feel quite calm about the future, and have done since being aware that I was aware smile emoticon I don't have fear as I know what takes place is what has to take place, and I have an acceptance that I am here to help others who may struggle with the transition. You can't be scared if you need to lend strength to others smile emoticon Q

CC: My entire future was a concern post or during the awakening.. The main reason, as I see it now, was that I did not know what my purpose was and I was totally confused.. I came across a website where the Author had written a lot helpful posts about the phases of an awakening but was insistent on the fact that there was 'no purpose ' post the awakening..That did not help matters.. I finally found a foothold when I found my purpose.. That's why it's so important to have open and free communication with like minded souls during the awakening process and that's exactly what this Council provided for me. God bless all the kindred souls that are part of this wonderful council !

AS: I'm going to love posting this one!.
　　What you call the past and what you call the future is all created from the NOW.. there is no future or past.. TIME... think about how slow you are going right now stuck behind this concept of time..Tick Toc Tick Toc:))

Scared of a future? No... Scared of not taking responsibility that you are the architect of YOUR so called future maybe...Accountability is a fear right?. It's not believing you can accomplish something so you don't take the step.. Well your future, if you truly think right now about it is, created NOW.. so is the imagery of your past as you live it right NOW..all of it is now.. So be afraid of not facing yourself, instead of some out force coming to harm you in some way or another..Oh and remember this is solely MY OPINION on how I see it.. How anyone else perceives it is there as well!!!

TWV: I suppose my biggest concern is that there's too much time and not enough time at the exact same time

Q7: What do you feel is preventing more souls from awakening and learning about their own path?

AB: I feel alignment with Krishnamurti who suggests it is thought. Thought is always limited, thus creates division, conflict and suffering.

KR: Fear of the unknown.

QQ: My personal feeling is that this is not the lifetime where they are supposed to do so. For many souls reincarnated right now, this life is about learning and growing within a personality, rather than tapping into or being conscious of the energies around them.
Anyone who feels the calling of soul or spirit finds it nearly impossible to ignore, but free will allows us to do so. If that free will is determined by fear or superstition, then I believe it is our role to show them how to live an awakened life without such limits, to show how it is possible to connect the personality, soul and spirit as one to live a life full of purpose and service to humanity. But, we have to also respect the free will of others if they decide that now is not the right time

JH: Fear and ego (sense of self and separateness)

GL: I think part of the reason most people aren't waking up is because most people do not research or ask questions. Most people just accept what they've been told; which is ironic considering the fact that we are taught to believe in lies as children. We are told that there is a Santa Claus, Tooth Fairy, Easter Bunny, etc. After growing older we come to discover that they are just fun fairy tale characters to make things fun and interesting. You would think that people would question everything that they've been told since we've been lied to by our parents from the beginning. Just something to think about.

MW: Money creates separation, the elite are brilliant at putting out disinformation and keeping us numbed to violence via movies tv shows and such. I believe in a personal level the only reason would be to fail to see love in the moment. In my humble opinion

LDJ: Fear. Fear to face the unknown. Fear of what others think of you. Fear, Fear, Fear of whatever is holding one back to make the next step.

SN: I believe the long years of conditioning in society makes people scared of what will happen to them if they follow their own paths. We been conditioned by society to follow orders and the status quo in order to survive. We fear to speak out on our own views and opinions about reality and don't want to be labeled as "crazy". Souls follow other's paths instead of realizing that they themselves are their own path to the true. We are all one conciousness experiencing itself, but we all have to walk different paths to our own truths. Also I believe mass media has played a huge role on the way we think and perceive the world, many great things started happening in my life the moment I stopped watching the news and started seeing my world they my own eyes and not what was on TV.

PW: I believe a vast majority of people go about like "sheep" being herded...they don't question the path, they just follow blindly along, doing what they've been told to do, believing what they've been told to believe.

It could be fear that stops them from breaking free, or it could be that it's just easier to follow along.

JBM: Because of the religions, many people slaves in their faith. People are lazy to search or to look in their own path. because they are always waiting what are the promises given by their Pastor, Priest with their scriptures.

ZW; I believe they didn't choose this path when they decided to live in this 3D world. They're probably not ready as they have yet to feel/live moments to become the being they chose for themselves. Each of us have different paths to navigate so that when we are ready to converge, we will combine all our different experiences to be whole. Have a good day

AB: From my own humble experience, I've somehow noticed various synchronicities that have arisen from time to time in my life, in some quite unexpected and unlikely ways. These events generally cause me to speculate from the seemingly automatic thoughts that arise as a consequence of them. These causes and the associated automatic thought effects would seem to be outside of my control or awareness, as though some hidden 'other' had seemingly quietly and deliberately brought about these synchronicities by design (or at least perhaps caused me to have thoughts of noticing them). I speculate further that this 'other' may in fact be the same 'thing' responsible for both providing sudden leaps of higher awareness in certain individuals at certain times, but for whatever reason may also deliberately cause others to remain occluded. Perhaps an individual awakening is like a bit part in some incomprehensible grander holistic plan or living process, in a similar way to how cells activate, become specialised or remain dormant at certain predetermined stages of growth within an organism. Perhaps we are like stem cells waiting for some cue to specialize. Another speculation of mine is that perhaps we are being tested by whatever this 'other' is, to see if we can recognise the tricks that it is playing on us, sort of like its running a simulation in order that we may help it work out, by trial an error, new creative innovations or strategy's that it may then weave into some grander evolution or purpose. Perhaps collectively we are this living entity. Whether we know it or not perhaps makes no difference at that higher level in the same way as a taste bud cell is unaware of our reaction to facebook! It serves its purpose well within the collective without this higher awareness. These are all just my humble speculations. I somehow feel drawn to question and ponder things trying to make sense of my own perception of reality and true nature though can just as easily throw these theories out. I'm also aware from experience that these thoughts may be transcended beyond description. I humbly offer this to maybe illustrate the endless possibilities from one in a unique state of occlusion such as mine. I can even speculate that such a maze of speculation and multiple false leads may also be what prevents others from finding further awareness

SS: Labels and affiliations. Cognitive dissonance and excessive administration.

NH: Nothing smile emoticon each awakens at exactly the right moment!

RM; Many doesn't believe in themselves and that self doubt holds them back... I'm speaking from experience..... But once you realize you can do this.... Then you will have your awakening

CS: Tv radio and controlled media. Those asleep will believe the lies because the truth is to real. They don't want to know even if they know. They would rather blame others and make money instead of helping others. Greed, money, media, sex, drugs drives them to stay asleep

DJ: people are to scared to face the truth and to believe the unknown the think its safer that way so the wont face their sins and show the truth because they know if they do it will show how many flaws they have and dont wont to face them they just need audience

JJJ

DJW: When we choose to ask the right questions, we awaken more! If there is no need to ask these questions, we remain in our unawakened state! This 'need to question' often comes from trauma in peoples lives and if you have no trauma, then why would you question your comfort!

KJ: Nothing prevents one from awakening. We are on our journey, learning our lessons of fear, separation, abandonment, self doubt.... arising largely from the delusion of judgment.

We are all just where we need to be on this perfect journey.

It is our soul's natural momentum to move towards wholeness, freedom, peace.....with the amazing possibility of basking in divine love, and light, along this journey.

AW: Some people do not want to be awakened, or perhaps this lifetime is not theirs to awaken. It is not an easy path to tread.

CK: I'd hate to think it's so simple, but I sort of think it's the "look at the shiny item" generation. We've disconnected from nature....its always new iPads, shiny cars, shiny lives and shiny phones to take pictures of those lives. There's no denying the energy felt by grounding with the trees or dipping your toes in water....but those practices have been fading out. There's so much to distract ourselves from our own hurts, our struggles and hard lessons. We're able to tune out if we choose. Awakening is very emotional....its spiritual....you have to feel, you have to ache....to cocoon before flying. So, while I feel our society has prevented its own growth by providing dazzling entertainment and toys, I also see an influx of awakening that has started. Maybe as a species we got in our own way but now the shine is fading and we'll come back to our roots?

KJ: People often mistake enlightenment or awakening as a fixed destination or goal, a onetime phenomenon.... rather it is our inevitable ongoing process, as human beings... it is our birthright to be always evolving, reconnecting, remembering our inner light, over and over again, deeper and deeper, as the lessons continue to unfold. Whether people call it enlightenment, or a journey of spiritual awakening, or no label in particular, it is really all the same journey, of an inevitable spiritual unfolding.... as a flower grows from a seed, to a plant, to an exquisite radiant blossom, our journey is the same,...... granted we are all at different phases in our blossoming, and rather than a linear journey it is a spiraling, always ultimately moving towards the light, towards love.

ML: I think people around the world would benefit greatly from people like all of us here, and everyone else around the world, always speaking our minds, sharing our thoughts openly, in all situations, around all people, in the kindest and most caring, from the heart words, always spoken with respect. Disregarding any judgments with a gentle smile on the way.

It doesn't matter if they don't agree. Or don't like what they hear, or don't listen, or if they want to argue. Smile and let them know that you genuinely accept that they are free to their own views and opinions. And that you appreciate that they do what they do for what ever reason they do it. And leave it at that.

If we can show them that we are open about our ways, and that which we have come to believe, and show acceptance and true understanding in their ways. They are a lot more likely to be open minded and accepting of our ways. And may become quite interested in starting their own journey.

And with that, their subconscious will also know from that point... A different, acceptable and kind persons way. You accept them. They accept you. Start the ball moving.

Plant kind seeds always. Get people thinking outside the box. They appreciate it. Just don't expect them to be able to catch up on your years of learning overnight or in one session. It will most likely take them years as well.

So even just one simple open thoughtful passing comment made with gentle love and care for the all. Every little bit makes a difference to us ALL.

JL: Great question and wonderful answers. I think that it is in a large part due to the disconnect from one another which is maintained through our boundary-filled perceptions of the outside world. These separating perceptions hinder such feelings as empathy and compassion from growing, which are necessary components to begin to breakdown the barriers between one another and also between "you" and self.

DF: My answer is simple. I believe it has to do with vibration and time. Like the strings on a guitar vibration strong enough to move the string. String able to interpret vibration. In terms of time, I quote Edgar Cayce it will not happen until the passage of the time and the Half time. Which I believe started after the Tsunami in Indonesia

XR: I think it is the attachment to the ego and self importance which fills the channels only by releasing and clearing can one be truly in touch with their higher self and trust and full fill what we are truly here for

TJ: Fear

BBR: There seems to be an incredible force driving the lack of awakening of souls. I have a very in depth knowledge of diet and the mind/body and our societies general diet is terrible! My awakening increased 10 fold when I found out I was guten intolerant and that lead me to research food more and more and for 3 and a half years I've read everything I could about diet and the mind/body. I see it in the behavior of those with really terrible diets, their minds are nowhere near awakening. But there's much more to it than that. And that's a part of the other forces. I see our people in power, the elite, the media, the famous people, the government all driving to keep us in a state of fear, unhealthy living, uneducated, closed minded and divided. Then there is the destroying of our ancient artifacts. The intentional refusal to accept that our ideas of our past are not correct, that the messages of those ancient artifacts are being purposely kept from the public. There's so much we could learn from studying our past and the civilizations that fell. Graham Hancock is doing wonders in bringing this to light. There is so much conditioning of the mind from such an early age and I'm fighting to overrule mine and keep my children from falling for it. The conditioning of the public school system is horrendous to see from the view of an awakened soul. I literally have to unteach my children. The emphasis on getting a job so you can buy things and have this and that is so strong. We are taught words like successful mean having lots of "nice" things. The pollution of our drinking water, the chemicals in our every day products, foods with who knows what in it, vaccines worry me, although I can't say I know they are or are not poisoning us, but the stories of the holistic doctors in Florida coming up dead because they had proof of what they are doing to us with the vaccines is scary. There is an intentional force keeping us down. Why is the question

Q8: What would be your advice, to give to a soul, that perhaps feels lost and disconnected from their path?

KS: I wouldn't give advice at all, I mean unless they specifically ask for it and then my answer would depend on the question. After all, how would I know where or why they feel the disconnect. This is a part of their journey. So I would just continue to shine my light alongside them and hope that one day it may help or at least give hope that they will one day lead themselves back.

MN: Get creative. Painting, writing, photography, dance, sports ect. Doing something you get lost in, maybe it's a passion from your past that you haven't done forever. Or perhaps a new creative outlet you want to try for the first time. Being creative allows the soul to speak to you and through you.

QQ: I have people such as this find me, specifically for that reason. I provide them with protection to rebalance them, then work with them and my various guides to help them find their answer. Even if they cannot connect with their soul, I am able to and so can join the dots for them to get them back on track

JT: I'm actually trying to help such an individual at the moment. I'd say meditation. Energy healing such as Reiki and crystal therapy. And meaning centered coaching. Perhaps an Akashic Records reading? Like Kimberly, what I won't do is handing out answers because they won't register on the emotional level which will render them practically useless. The soul has to do the "soul searching" as part of the journey. But yes definitely engulf them in love and healing light so they can find the strength within themselves to confront whatever they need to confront

SS: I would tell them "you're in a great position. Now you know what it's like to be lost or not on your path. You wouldn't have that feeling unless you somehow knew there was a path to be walked. You are not alone and there is guidance waiting to help you. Ask the Holy One, your Inner Guidance, for help and to show you what to do. But most importantly, ask how to better hear it's voice and follow it's guidance. And when you forget, ask again...and again...and again. It's not going to abandon you, because it is "Inner" Guidance. And not only does it go with you wherever you go, it goes before you to prepare your way."

MN: Recognizing that you are not connected and you know that you're not living in the way you desire, is half the recipe for getting back into your soul work. It is within the focused attention of lacking passion that your highest self is speaking to you. And so just by beginning to ask for advice or taking some kind of action towards changing the current direction, your precious light has started glowing brighter already. So, give thanks, Whoo hoo!!!!!! For just by showing up your on your path

AB: As perhaps more of a person seeking pointers myself, I would say the best kind of advice I have received that resonated most strongly with me has been where another has honestly shared the detailed sequence of 'ordinary' steps or events that led to some 'extraordinary' insight. For me, words of advice describing extraordinary perceptions can appear tantalizing and motivating but sometimes frustratingly empty. Although the construct of words may make sense, the packaged knowledge they contain can remain elusive to the inexperienced receiver. Someone who's lost I think needs signposts they can relate to at their level rather than descriptions of extraordinary higher levels. I find there's something about personal human stories that resonate more with me than mechanical descriptions of what to do, or not do. I also sometimes think advice must be first sought rather than just given to be received with the greatest impact.

SMB: Follow the energy, if you follow your highest vibration without questioning why it will always lead you to where you're supposed to be. Don't overthink it, thinking is for the physical self, the energy at it's highest vibration is the path of the spiritual self.

SE: My advice, would be a path of least resistance (well... for people I associate with I guess). NERDS.

Brush up on some Buddhism, brush up on some metaphysics.

More generally, try and always make something a learning experience, and always try and make it a positive experience.

TVF: Initial advice = breathe! Breathe in, breathe out. To stabilize, you! In this life we must breathe first and foremost to sustain life, calming, minimize the stress response (also known as Fight or Flight, and in recent years fight, flight, freeze) These are natural responses to survival. Even in animals. Just... breathe! This is the best beginning I can offer for a lost or disconnect soul because once a person can find their "even or pole" in body, mind and spirit they can move forward. (I remind myself often)

MJU: No matter where you are doubt will travel with you. Its your teacher.

DC: Awareness..Not advice, more my experience of it..I can look back now, at the start, or the moment I was aware of disconnecting-although I could feel internal changes happening, it's only now i can look back and see, although my changes were the wakening point for me and, that brought a lot of the emotional chaos (I experienced) fragmenting part of me! I think my experience will be different to anyone else's, my understanding only come from that experience. What is really apparent to me now about that process is its happening:) just be aware of it, the feel of it, exceptance of t -through that feeling. only after that I learned to divert any thoughts rational, logic,)ego! was in full affect, the energy of those thoughts were noticeable to the emotional chaos and disconnect I was already feeling.. Being creative, reading, talking to people that understood, crystals, oils, etc..everything everyone recommends is key! Through that you discover something that's for you, that resonates with you..The reason I feel that's important is..you will have what you need to help you, around you in some way already! However it presents its self for you - is your own awareness of it..In the chaos trust the Universe flight that is around you..be aware of what!!

TJ: Remember that there ALWAYS is a path & as long as we trust in the Divine we will always be on it, it may just be wider than our point of view! Broader than our eyes can see or our mind can comprehend. But as long as we keep trudging along, trusting, we will end up exactly where we are supposed to be!!

KR: There are as many different paths as people... And everything is unfolding just as it is meant to. Trust in yourself and the rest will follow.

Q9: How do you envisage the future of this planet, in 100 years time & why?

AB: I find it hard to imagine. In a conventional 3D reality sense, if we can shrug off the dark ideas of geopolitical threats to peace, then extrapolating from the technology to date, I feel the ideas around information technology will extend into virtual reality, a world of connected sensors, robotic automation and artificial intelligence will all blend together to create a hyper connected global society, enabling much greater sharing of knowledge and skills, as well as goods and services, in unimaginably creative ways. I think drone technology for example will advance to something akin to an avatar for people to virtually control, explore and experience, as if they were there in remote or hostile environments beyond whats possible for the physical body to cope. I think this explosion in interconnections and shared knowledge will also allow us to drop our misinformed prejudices and see how similar we all are in our ambition. To realise how much more we can accomplish together for mutual benefit rather than letting a tiny controlling few keep us all divided to profit from our endless labour. Out of necessity, I think the idea of unelected power such as multinational corporations and their conflict of interest profit will be banned and natural resources globally will be more carefully and sustainably managed through automated feedback systems monitoring supply and demand. Automation I think will play a big role in things like farming and delivery of goods in the most efficient manner possible. I think artificial intelligence and algorithms will play a big role in for example making economic exchange mechanisms and systems of law and governance tamper proof, transparent and decentralised to reduce the tendency for corruption and to promote trust. I think all these physical opportunities for greater awareness and knowledge will also force us look at ourselves in different ways, to question and look much deeper within, promoting a shared spiritual evolution. Where that may lead is beyond my imagining

FA: Humans living with no imperfections, Health issues no longer existent. Average life spans ranging into thousands of years. Complete global common objectives of nothing other than love for each other and expansion threw technologies being learnt threw our ascension threw higher dimensions (as a result of a balanced mind spirit and soul) Very Similar to the times of Lemurians.

JJJ

Those that have chosen to bail on earth and start a new society on
    Mars in fear of what our tiny understanding of astral threat levels of today have taught them.

I believe shortly, *very* shortly there judgement of science vs spirituality will prove them wrong *right before there eyes*
    Karma.
    A.G

DM: i agree that the time of mass transition is beginning and coming and will only increase with time

TVF: 100 years from now = not far enough. For us, the ability to ascend reinforces our higher existence/ eternal, but with time comes others knowing we can, and another responsibility to protect what we could potentially be wiped away for as human beings. Paranoid? Not at all, just reserved

DM: for me personally i believe and think that consciousness will find its way and that we will become more and more aware of ourselves and the amount of people that are connecting to the divine will increase in turn beginning to formulate a reality with a society that aims at self discovery and expansion of ones awareness and knowledge of what is etc. i think this because of visions i saw in an experience i had, of humans elevating and coming together which led further generations to ascend and live in peace

LDJ: For the future is already here and yet it isn't. I hope in the future from this timeline that there will be peace and the balance of everything is restored. I hope that this will happen, yet it is still a matter of the choices of people. Do they make a choice by intuition or the choice of the mind (fear). It is up to mankind now....The coming changes are good, yet I "fear" that many people will think that things are done at that moment and I already know that it is not. We have to go further, move on, keep focusing on restoring the balance. It will take a lot of more years before the balance will be restored and still...it depends on the choices of mankind .. It is not a matter of choosing sides...it is a matter of walking in the middle and to embrace both sides because both sides reside within. Reject one of those and one itself won't be in balance. Balance is key... (all of this how it appears to me at this now moment)

QQ: I believe that the karmic balancing that we are currently seeing will continue, with the Mother Earth and the vibrational levels we are only just becoming aware of, taking precedence over the current physical manifestations. The free will of all souls means that our response to that may change, but the change to gaia must and will continue. Q

AM: I believe with certainty that we will collectively be on a higher plane. Maybe not ultimate enlightenment, for the human existence is a never-ending lesson, but operating on a comparatively higher consciousness. More and more, I see the mindfulness movement making its way across society, becoming more mainstream. People are becoming more aware. Energies are shifting.

CK: I hope that in this amount of time we've stopped searching without and start searching within. Our souls see each other without the mask of our bodies, our hearts feel each other beat and our minds open up, unlocking the secrets of the past stored within. We stop funding useless wars, mindless gadgets, and the promotion of greed. We're now caring for each other, pour our thoughts into the planet and into those surviving here. We live with the universal law of respect.....there would be no need for other laws. No need for the state consuming money because it will have no value~

SMB: Sadly I think the divide will be greater...There will be more enlightenment on one side and even more greed and excess on the other. I see a real struggle with those that seek to destroy the very habitat which sustains us. I hope I'm wrong.

ZG: Energetic.

Dynamic.,...Changing.

A change I do not predict most of humanity will be able to keep pace with.

ZW: in 100 years, humanity has been freed of our self imposed shackles and limitations and we live in harmony with other beings on this planet and have clear communications with all beings including those of higher vibrational densities. That was why we had come to this place at this time, for this to come true, and I believe we will succeed in doing so.

AD: Well I believe we are going through a massive transition and it's been going on for quite some time. Basically the divine light and the universe will give us two choices in how we will shape our future.. A) live as we are right now or B) wake up and learn that we are all connected... Depending on what happens within the next few years will shape our future. I have hope for humanity but they need a lot of work and those willing to change will make a better world.

Q10: What advice to other souls would you give, in order to help find their inner balance, and inner calm

TM: From my perspective I would tell these souls, to find a quiet place where they can be physically comfortable. Closing their eyes and clearing their mind of all questions, thoughts and fears. As long as it takes for their mind to become void of these ideas, to focus their mind on a point of light in their consciousness and feel their astral selves rise into this feeling of "oneness" where they can find balance within themselves and be connected to the source, of love and light. This is the place where they can find their true purpose. L&L~

AB: Purge ego and expectations. Freedom of thought is to be free of thoughts. Live in the never ending moment of now. Be paying attention to all that is around you, with out judgement. Just learn to be.

DR: You are how the Universe is becoming aware of itself. You are how the the Cosmos is realizing it's own existence. Any feelings of inner chaos, any feelings of unbalance are direct results from forgetting that you are much broader than what resides within your body. You are an individual reflection of everything you see and experience.

As Thomas is recommending, meditation can be instrumental in bringing a soul back into alignment. He also recommends focal points which in themselves are great but you concentrating on anything is not important. In fact, I feel releasing a hold on all thoughts would be much more beneficial. This itself can be a bit challenging to someone who has never thought about not thinking. It's something that we've been led to believe we can't NOT do. For those individuals who may be new to releasing mental images I always recommend they focus on their breathing. Actually visualize your diaphragm expanding and contracting with each breath. Soon you will begin to realize that as you bring your focus onto your personal connection point with the all that's All, you are not able to focus on anything else you feel is a problem in your experience. That's what your looking for!

Now, I've found that as I release the grip of my ego and allow the Universe to have its way with my consciousness it has a way of rearranging reality to match my true inner vibration.

Never forget, you are Love and you are also loved.

KB: Exploring every religion or worshiping ideals and the reasons why societies participated in them furthers understanding of the inner self. I believe that souls become more understanding when they review chakras and their origins as well as what they were used for even if they only use in ways that works for them. I just believe that exploring the realms of every 'positively' designed system and focusing on how to apply it to your inner peace helps vastly. When you are able to view yourself as a decision making machine, In a sense, then you are able to access consciousness that awakens inner to experience outer more intensely.

This is only if resistance is high for souls. Often this length is not fully needed. I introduce myself to myself everyday so that I can know that the affirmations I give myself are true and will be applied throughout the day. When one is even slightly interested in enlightenment, all they need is something they can relate to! Everyone's stories can help

nner balance also pertains to identifying perceived distortions that are stressors and knowing that we are one with ourselves so we can be more of a one with everything. Life's tests try to leave us bounded and breathless but you are free and we are saved from distortion of fear residing in ego. We have overcome the false reality and perceived consciousness in realms unheard of. We are love and love is us. United we are much love and let loves light shine through for a new life, skies graced us with new air rising to a new heir of conscious revolution of minds in the earth that is one. (Poem)

MJU: I would tell them to find a page Like this. So many different ways, one will fit just right

KR: Good grounding practice eg. yoga or meditation. Something practical to remain grounded!! Highly important when trying to bring the spirit to the earthly plane in order to remain "human"

JT: Accept that in this realm, storms are part of the process. There is no positive or negative experience, there is only experience. Our spirits are eternal and infinite, we can neither be harmed nor destroyed. Ultimately, we are here to experience the totality of our creative and divine nature as the One. May as well have a little fun and a diverse experience, right? Eternity and "nothing but light" does get a little boring "up there." Lol.

AM: Learn to love solitude. Finding balance comes in silent moments of listening to your humming, vibrant essence. Focusing on your center, everything else falls into place.

RLM: Don't try to stop your thoughts. Don't try to control. Watch and listen to your thoughts and feelings. Realize that you are not your thoughts and your feelings, you are the witness to them. Honor them, accept them, but don't identify with them. They are experiences given to you.

CK: My advice would be learning to filter out the noise around you. It will come at you from every angle and a good place to start would be simple meditations to clear the outside world traffic. Take just 15 minutes a day for you, only you, to work on your quiet time. Learn to sit and clear all thoughts, restrict movement and just be. Realize that the noise is there to distract you from the depths your mind is capable of reaching. Whether this be from our natural behavior as humans or a higher plot to distract us, it's the only way to calm the waves of your heart and mind. When you find that small moment where you're free from the shackles of thought and movement of doing… peace will be granted so you can learn the feeling of calm. Then build on it… try for 20 minutes…. then longer… it's beautifully calm

JBM: Imagine how free, relieved and happy you would be, if you could stay calm and poised in the midst of whatever is happening in your life. Learn to let go, stop taking everything too personally, and avoid getting upset by what people say and do.

QQ: Inner balance requires outer balance - you cannot have one without the other. To be calm on the inside, you must be calm on the outside. If your current physical manifestation (who you are in this lifetime) has an environment which is chaotic, noisy, confusing, jumbled or unclean, then whatever inner calm can be achieved will become an escape from that reality which is so challenging. That in itself is no longer inner calm or inner balance.

By focusing on calming down and simplifying your external life, you will create a pure, powerful and rich foundation for your inner energies to flourish. Beautiful flowers cannot grow in untended soil.

This ultimately means that you have to look at every element of your existence, appraise it honestly and authentically to see whether it is working for you or against you and take steps to correct it. Whilst doing so, enrich your understanding of the inner working of the soul with whatever literature, concepts, theories or people that you feel connected to, so that once the outside is calm, the transition to an inner calm will have already begun

ZW: by far, the most difficult one for me as I'm still grappling to find inner peace, most times. I'm a very emotional person and I get triggered fast by others' responses and reactions. I work at a chaotic environment, full of people, so it's easy for me to lose my cool. But I've learnt that taking controlled breaths help, temporarily at least. The best way for me to achieve inner peace is to go to nature, take long walks, be near water and just breathe. I don't meditate but I'm sure meditation will help too

HI: Well, first of all I would offer a session with special focus to reconnect to him/her soul & higher self. If this is not done at first, it will be very difficult to reach inner balance & to be calm.

After this initiation a daily focus on meditation (e.g. breathing love in & stress out, conscious focus to soul & higher self aso) in silent or with special music like Delta, Theta, Alpha waves aso, will rise the inner balance step by step.

And of course... practice makes perfect

AB: Everyone receives advice differently. I admit I often think the 'spiritual speak' of others is like listening to opera. It sounds lovely, seems to contain beautifully evocative elements, but honestly sometimes can't understand or recognise a word of it to comprehend or be able to internalise the significance of subtle meaning in whats being said and intended!

If I were to somehow go back and give my younger self some practical advice, it would be to not cling so tightly to cherished beliefs and be prepared to throw them out with new realisations and paradigm shifts in perception. Follow and trust your intuition. Question everything, even mundane assumptions upon which beliefs are founded and notice the tendency to defend beliefs! Take more neutral note of even the contrary perceptions of others, and think of them more as pieces within a wider jigsaw to be able to start to notice emerging underlying patterns of a subtle action at play. Notice also what's not said! Spend more time in the moment observing just being whilst going about day to day normal activities, as well as taking more time out for quiet reflection to observe the source and effects of thoughts. Have more tolerance, forgiveness and acceptance of the unique perceptions of others. Be more grateful

TP: Breathe. Knowing everything doesn't matter. Dont rush anything. Enjoy the moment always

DC: I had to ponder on this a little, as my advice is merely a contribution!based on my own personal experiences..inner calm/inner balance, and this processing was the most challenging for me. At the start I would say my awareness was not as it is now-I didn't find any of the conventional methods for meditating that worked for me, or finding a clam to centre myself, I know now the importance of trying different routes-as well as listening to others who offer advice, while they may not have the same experience as you they certainly understand the processing your experiencing! Don't disregard anything would be my advice, for my experience as I grew, was I did in fact return to certain things- that did help! For example, I was introduced to crystals early on due to the fact my aunt realised what I was experiencing was more about energies, and not like her own or my grandmothers take on it which was more the spiritual path of mediumship for spirit so my balance and calm had to be explored, for me to find my own tune/frequency that worked for me:) crystals at the time I couldn't even be near as they amplified my energies so I was not ready yet, however I returned to them as I grew, and had more awareness of the inner mechanics of my own internal system. My understanding of it now with no doubt, was to recognise that everything I would need to help me on my path was being provided - but not necessarily for me at that time:) this process changed as I grew, finding my inner calm and balance was, and is something that changes as I do! Of coarse now-I trust the universe as it knows something I don't, and constantly provides what you need, when you need it:) If I could explain in my reality, would be to describe the universe as the air traffic control tower-was your heading home, logged on-a flight path opens up for your route smile emoticon my process was I needed to go inward and spend time with me..solitude is were my calm and balance was understood! Don't worry, or over think anything, pay attention to everything that comes your way-hit or miss is irrelevant, what's relevant is to try, take note and move on from it. I find now when the storm comes, my inner calm / balance needs can change at each stage!this can be something new or something simple -that is for us each to explore individual to our personal journey:) simple tidying up with headphones on is my thing, something I have always done:) difference now is I see it's actually a form of meditation, calm, a focus were I'm still, quiet..remembering basic, simple things you've always done that seems to be mundane tasks' which I really didn't like-during stormy times this mundane place can be the calm.confusing and difficult as our journey s can be sometimes! One thing for sure is, the storms are growth, the person who walked in it-won't be the person that comes out of it..Its all good

FA: I would personally advise them to try and block out any issues, stresses, problems ect from there mind and simply lay down, relax, breath, and focus on the moment and nothing else. No thoughts of anything to do with something whether it be in the next 5 second, 12 hours, next week ect. Literally concentrate on you right at the present, And enjoy the feeling of nothingness and calmness.

TSF: One way of finding balance is to visualize your whole being as a sphere- both your physical body, and the space around it. Imagine that within this sphere are an infinite number of axes, crisscrossing in every direction possible, and all meeting at an infinitesimally small point, right in the centre of your heart.

These axes are the polarities that exist within each of us: big picture thinking vs. detailed analysis; pride in oneself vs. care for the collective; focus on emotion vs. focus on action. These, of course, are only examples, as the potential polarities that exist within our being are truly endless.

Our goal is to learn to dance on that nearly nonexistent point; to be so evenly spread between polarities that it is as though we simply float in the middle of our being, perfectly balanced and buoyed by the equal push and pull of every endpoint surrounding our sphere of being.

Understand that while it seems that issues, problems, and concerns come from without, everything that "happens to us" is really just designed to give us the opportunity to examine our own reaction to that issue, problem, or concern.

When we are given these opportunities, we can learn to move our reactions and responses closer to our centre along each axis, with the ultimate goal of becoming centred and balanced in our own being.

CC: I don't really have any advice. For me it's a journey that I am still on.. I can only say one thing.. just try and let go.. The process of awakening is one that sets you free of all ties and attachments.. even the attachment to our own existence.. The more we try to hold on, the harder it is..

Q11: If you could know the answer, to any one single question, what would the question be, and why would you seek the answer to that specific question?

FA: f every person, thing, energy, planet.. everything known to our level of existence is all in fact the same one thing (like a thorn bush, with every little spike being the different things we perceive as something else. I would seek the answer to that question to confirm whether finally the full enlightenment of all has been achieved, or if there there is much more too it

JJJ

CS: Why r we here? Because it will make life real

AC: i would like to know: how we came from the 'SOURCE" and who we are. we have lost connection with this and every day people fall back into carkness. this has been quite the puzzle for me.knowing self and purpose is one thing but knowing how and who would help us better understand i think. it fascinates me when i look at people and see just how small and special we are just on earth alone and we have a brain thats partly used to it's full potential and hearts that have no limit to the ultimate love yet we put up walls. there has to be a reason. a real reason why we are capable of loving so much but dont, having the ultimate connection with each other and life but we dont and using the full use of our brains but we dont? who are we? how did we come from 'the source"?

SO: Why are we worshiping things outside of us when 'All that is' is within us. Why are we worshiping the source when we are actually part of it. How is it that we don't remember being one before being born. What is the sense to all of this?

MN: I'd want to know the sense of it. Of course there may not be any. It's just chaos and we're all a part of it! Or it's all divine and we're all a part of it. I've just come to peace with the fact that we exist.

MJU: s there intelligent existence after death? I'm 68. pretty good reason

SD: Whether the seemingly unique creation that can happen in ones mind and imagination is a contained occurrence; restricted within the respective mind of the one who thought it. OR is it the collective rememberence of past ages, times...futures? Or even, the creation of alternate planes, alternate lives...a processor and builder of the universes we cohabitate.

I've been wondering often about this because as an artist who builds their creative world; making rules, pantheons, souls and worlds as I draw them...they often feel too real, even too independent to only be a contained within my mind and only thoughts.

AB: What is the true nature and potential of my existence? I feel KNOWING this would allow me to BE, ACT and CREATE in the most beneficial way possible.

JRB: I have many of the same questions listed here. My version would be to know the true nature of my soul/ higher self/past incarnations in this time & space while being part of Source, connected to all other living beings & the relationship to multidimensional realities in the physical realm (by that I mean as opposed to a spiritual plane). Is there one "true reality" outside the ones we create in a particular time, space & within our own minds? We seem to incarnate to learn & progress on a soul level that relates back to our spiritual lives without physical bodies. I am curious as to how other versions of ourselves play out in alternate dimensions & how they are interconnected & effect each other. I would ask this because as I learn more about our universe this has been crossing my mind frequently. I would use this knowledge to be the best version of myself in order to help others who want to become more enlightened on their journey on this planet.

QQ: What would utter spiritual peace feel like? In our physical form we are unable to connect fully as our spirit body, although there are many mechanisms known to us that allow a tantalising hint towards it. But to know what Source truly feels like, where the ability to be energy and be light and be everything is the norms and without the encumbrances of a physical form, would be magical. This is what we strive for in our attempts at linking with our souls and our spirit energies, and it is the connection we all feel deep within that makes us sure that what we seek exists if we can but only find our ways back.
    Why? Because I want to go home.

Printed in Great Britain
by Amazon